100 Days with Jesus

100 Days with Jesus

Dr. Elmer Towns

© Copyright 2019–Elmer Towns

All rights reserved. This book is protected by the copyright laws of the United States of America. This book may not be copied or reprinted for commercial gain or profit. The use of short quotations or occasional page copying for personal or group study is permitted and encouraged. Permission will be granted upon request. Unless otherwise identified, Scripture quotations are taken from the New King James Version. Copyright © 1982 by Thomas Nelson, Inc. Used by permission. All rights reserved. Scripture quotations marked NLT are taken from the Holy Bible, New Living Translation, copyright 1996, 2004, 2015. Used by permission of Tyndale House Publishers., Wheaton, Illinois 60189. All rights reserved. Scripture quotations marked TLB are taken from The Living Bible; Tyndale House, 1997, © 1971 by Tyndale House Publishers, Inc. Used by permission. All rights reserved. Scripture quotations marked KJV are taken from the King James Version. Scripture quotations marked AMP are taken from the Amplified® Bible, Copyright © 2015 by The Lockman Foundation, La Habra, CA 90631. All rights reserved. Used by permission. Scripture quotations marked TLB are taken from The Living Bible; Tyndale House, 1997, © 1971 by Tyndale House Publishers, Inc. Used by permission. All rights reserved. Please note that Destiny Image's publishing style capitalizes certain pronouns in Scripture that refer to the Father, Son, and Holy Spirit, and may differ from some publishers' styles.

DESTINY IMAGE® PUBLISHERS, INC.

P.O. Box 310, Shippensburg, PA 17257-0310

"Promoting Inspired Lives."

This book and all other Destiny Image and Destiny Image Fiction books are available at Christian bookstores and distributors worldwide.

For more information on foreign distributors, call 717-532-3040.

Reach us on the Internet: www.destinyimage.com.

ISBN 13 TP: 978-0-7684-4669-2

ISBN 13 eBook: 978-0-7684-4670-8

ISBN 13 HC: 978-0-7684-4672-2

ISBN 13 LP: 978-0-7684-4671-5

For Worldwide Distribution, Printed in the U.S.A.

1 2 3 4 5 6 7 8 / 23 22 21 20 19

Contents

Preface Discover Me VIII
Author's note X
1. I Am Jesus Your Shepherd (Jehovah Roi) 1
2. I Am Jesus Christ Your Lord.. 3
3. I Am Jesus the Image of the Invisible God........................ 5
4. I Am Jesus: Worthy 7
5. I Am Jesus, the All and In All... 9
6. I Am Jesus, the Young Child 11
7. I Am Jesus the Triumphant Lamb..................................... 13
8. I Am Jesus the Unspeakable Gift 15
9. I Am Jesus Savior 17
10. I Am Jesus Rabboni 19
11. I Am Jesus the Carpenter's Son 21
12. I Am the Lord Jesus Christ 23
13. I Am Jesus Rabbi 25
14. I Am Jesus the Precious One 27
15. I Am Jesus My Name Is Wonderful 29
16. I Am Jesus, the Preeminent One 31
17. I Am Jesus the Way 33
18. I Am Jesus the True Vine.. 35
19. I Am Jesus the Door Of The Sheep 37
20. I Am Jesus the Bread of God 39
21. I Am Jesus the Truth 41
22. I Am Jesus the Light 43
23. I Am Jesus My Name Is Powerful 45
24. My Name Jesus Is Above Every Name 47
25. I Am Jesus a More Excellent Name.................................. 49

Contents

26. I Am Jesus a Column of Smoke and Fire 51
27. I Am Jesus the Son of Joseph 53
28. I Am Jesus Immanuel (God with Us) 55
29. I Am Jesus the Great I Am 57
30. I Am Jesus the Anointed of God 59
31. I Am Jesus the Chief Cornerstone.. 61
32. I Am Jesus Your Lord... 63
33. I Am Jesus the Lamb 65
34. I Am Jesus a Sacrifice to God 67
35. I Am Jesus Ruler 69
36. I Am Jesus a Stone Cut Out of the Mountain................................. 71
37. I Am Jesus a Man Approved By God... 73
38. I Am Jesus the Lord Strong and Mighty.. 75
39. I Am Jesus the Savior of the Body 77
40. I Am Jesus a Merciful and Faithful High Priest 79
41. I Am Jesus the One Who Has the Bride.. 81
42. I Am Jesus, the Holy One and Just... 83
43. My Name Jesus Is a Powerful Name.. 85
44. I Am Jesus the Word 87
45. I Am Jesus the Author of Your Faith... 89
46. I Am Jesus the One Who Comes Down from Heaven.................. 91
47. I Am Jesus the Fruit of Mary's Womb... 93
48. I Am Jesus the One Who Sanctifies 95
49. I Am Jesus the Babe.. 97
50. I Am Jesus a Star Out of Jacob.. 99
51. I Am Jesus a Righteous Man 101
52. I Am Jesus a Refiner's Fire... 103
53. I Am Jesus a Ransom for Many 105
54. I Am Jesus a Stronghold in the Day of Trouble 107

55. I Am Jesus Your Strong Consolation 109
56. I Am Jesus the Salvation of God 111
57. I Am Jesus the Bearer of Sin 113
58. I Am Jesus a Teacher Come from God 115
59. I Am Jesus a Sweet-Smelling Aroma 117
60. I Am Jesus the Sun of Righteousness 119
61. I Am Jesus the Seed of Abraham 121
62. I Am Jesus the Savior of the World 123
63. I Am Jesus the Fountain of Life 125
64. I Am Jesus the Forerunner 127
65. I Am Jesus the Firstborn 129
66. I Am Jesus Undefiled 131
67. I Am Jesus the Son of God 133
68. I Am Jesus Son of the Father 135
69. I Am Jesus Son of the Living God 137
70. I Am Jesus the Son Who Is Consecrated for Evermore 139
71. I Am Jesus the Resurrection 141
72. I Am Jesus the Testimony of God 143
73. I Am Jesus the Triumphant Son of Man 145
74. I Am Jesus the Trustworthy Witness 147
75. I Am Jesus Faithful and True 149
76. I Am Jesus the Only Wise God 151
77. I Am Jesus the Prince of the Kings of the Earth 153
78. I Am Jesus the Righteous Judge 155
79. I Am Jesus the Only Begotten of the Father 157
80. I Am Jesus the Light of the Glorious Gospel 159
81. I Am Jesus the Light of the Knowledge of the
    Glory of God 161
82. I Am Jesus the Lion of the Tribe of Judah 163

Contents

83. I Am Jesus the Lord of Glory 165
84. I Am Jesus the Lord of Peace 167
85. I Am Jesus, the Man Christ Jesus 169
86. I Am Jesus the Judge of the Living and the Dead......................... 171
87. I Am Jesus the King Eternal 173
88. I Am Jesus the Foundation Which Is Laid.................................... 175
89. I Am Jesus, the Hope of Israel... 177
90. I Am Jesus the Commander of the Hosts of the Lord................. 179
91. I Am Jesus the Cloud.. 181
92. I Am Jesus the Consolation of Israel.. 183
93. I Am Jesus a Good Man 185
94. I Am Jesus the Lawgiver 187
95. I Am Jesus the Life.. 189
96. I Am Jesus the Lamb Slain from the Foundation
 of the World 191
97. I Am Jesus the Head of All Principality and Power.................... 193
98. I Am Jesus, the Rock... 195
99. I Am Jesus the Redeemer... 197
100. I Am Jesus the Head of the Body.. 199
Appendix 1 Jesus: Names, Titles, Metaphors, Figures of
 Speech and Pictures of Jesus 201
Appendix 2 Jesus: Preeminent Pronouns of Jesus in
 Scripture 233

Preface
Discover Me

I am Jesus, this book is about Me and My many names. Every day you will discover a new name or title about Me, and you will learn something new about Me. Then begin living what you learn.

I have over 700 different names in Scripture for Me, including titles, symbols, figures of speak, types and metaphors. Why so many? Because I do so many things; always acting, guiding, protecting, empowering, not to mention forgiving sin and offering salvation to those who call on Me. Technically, I have many more than 700 names, many you don't know yet, and many you will never know because humans are finite, I am infinite.

Only 100 of My names were chosen to be included in this book. These are the ones that might help you in your daily life. Some of these names—devotional—will help in your walk with Me. Other names are doctrinal, they will deepen your understanding of Me. Still other names are practical to broaden your Christian service. After you finish learning about Me through these 100 names, order the book, *Discover Me Through My Many Names*. It is an explanation of over 700 of My names, titles and symbols. You will learn more about Me through many of My names you've never known or studied.

Each name and title for a person represents a different aspect of their life. For instance, Elmer Towns, compiler of this book is called husband, father, grandfather, dean faculty, golfer, author, Sunday school teacher and so on. The more a person does, the more names and titles they have. Since I am greater than any human wouldn't you expect Me to have the most titles and names?

As you read through this devotional, you'll learn more about Me than ever before. As you explore many of My names, be prepared to know Me more intimately than ever before. And when you learn more about Me and My relationship to you, you'll learn more about yourself. Be prepared to come closer to Me than ever before.

Read carefully…read daily…read expectantly…and read in fellowship with Me.

As you read, reach out to touch Me. You will find that before you do, I'll be reaching out to you.

~Jesus

Author's note

These 100 devotionals were taken from the book, *The Names of Jesus*. That book examines over 700 of My names, titles, offices, descriptions and metaphors. Elmer Towns the author of the book is also the compiler for these devotionals. He originally taught 13 lesson on My names in the Pastor's Bible Class at Thomas Road Baptist Church (attendance 2,000 in 1987). Then he preached 13 sermons on My names at a deeper life meeting at Muskego Conference, Oakville, Ontario, Canada. Next, Towns wrote them into an adult Bible class study book that was issued by Gospel Light Sunday School Publications, Ventura, California, 1987. Towns is Co-Founder of Liberty University with Dr. Jerry Falwell Sr. His ability to organize Bible content into teachable truths was reflected in the early organizational structure of Liberty University and was the foundation that made Liberty University the largest Christian university in the world. The way these devotionals were used in the past is indicative of the influence they can leave on your life.

1
I Am Jesus Your Shepherd (Jehovah Roi)

The Lord is my shepherd; I shall not want.
—Psalm 23:1

I Am Jesus the Lord your Shepherd. In My life I identified Myself, "I am the Good Shepherd" (John 10:11). I am the Shepherd of Psalm 23 who can lead you to green pastures where you can lie down for rest. There you can feed on green grass to regain your strength. I can lead you beside still water to moisten your dry tongue. Will you follow Me today? I your Shepherd will lead you in the right paths, for My name's sake. I will guide you through shadows in death's valley. Don't be afraid of shadows, for they are only dark eclipses created by threatening mountains. I may lead you through dark valleys but never leave you there.

> *Shepherd, there are many paths calling to me. What is the best path for me today? Guide me. The mountain trails through life's valleys are filled with dead-end canyons. Don't let me get lost, help me.*

I your Shepherd will prepare a table of food for you after you get through your dark valley. Your favorite cup is full and running over. Eat, drink, and be thankful of My provisions. I your Shepherd have two "sheep dogs" to pursue you if you stray. The first is My goodness, to keep you following Me. The second is My mercy, to forgive any future wayward steps.

Shepherd, it feels good to rest happily beside You. When my eyes get distracted by the things of this world, draw me back with goodness and mercy. Shepherd, I want to dwell with You in Your house forever. Amen.

Reading: Psalm 23

Key Thoughts: I the Lord want a relationship with you.

2
I Am Jesus Christ Your Lord

I thank God—through Jesus Christ our Lord! So then, with the mind I myself serve the law of God, but with the flesh the law of sin.
—Romans 7:25

My name is *Jesus*. That's the personal name given to Me. The angel told Joseph to "Name Him Jesus for He will save His people from their sins" (Matt. 1:23). Throughout the gospels, people called Me *Jesus*. My office is *Christ*, much like people in the church has an office of minister or teacher. The office "Christ" in the Greek language is the word "Messiah" in Hebrew. It comes from the root that means "to anoint." When you say, Jesus Christ," you are saying, "Jesus the Anointed One." People were inaugurated into office in the Old Testament by anointing; they had oil poured over them—a symbol of prosperity and the Holy Spirit.

I approach You through your earthly name Jesus. I thank You for coming to Earth for me. I come to You through Your office Christ. You are the One who died for me.

My title is "Lord." Just as the executive leader of the United States has the title " president," I have the eternal title "Lord." With My title "Lord" goes ownership and control. Do I have control over your life? Also, this title gives Me authority to direct people under Me and to punish those who disobey My laws. Have you let Me direct your life? I am *Jesus Christ your Lord*; am I your personal Savior and Master?

> *Thank You, Jesus, for coming into my life to save me. Now I give You control of my life; I make You my Master. Jesus Christ, You are my Lord. Amen.*

Reading: Romans 10:1-17

Key Thought: I want to be saved by My redeeming name *Jesus*; pray through the power of My office, *Christ*, and submit to My authority in the *Lord*.

3
I Am Jesus the Image of the Invisible God

He is the image of the invisible God, the firstborn over all creation.
—Colossians 1:15

I am Jesus the *Image of the Invisible God* you can't see. Throughout history people have asked to see God, but they are protected. "No man shall see Me, and live" (Exodus 33:20). But there's another reason, You can't see God the Father, because there's nothing to see. I told the Samaritan woman, "God is Spirit" (John 4:24); and a spirit has no flesh or material substance to see. But still people want to see God. So they can see God by looking at Me. Read the pages of Scripture to see My character and miracles. See My acts of kindness. When you see Me in the Bible, you'll see God. You'll see how God in human flesh acted and reacted, for I am God. I'm the *Image of the Invisible God*.

*Lord Jesus, in the pages of Scripture, I see
kindness in Your face. I feel the forgiveness of
Your grace. When I can't see anything else, the
image of God I trace.*

An image is an exact reflection. The original object can't move without the same movement in the image. I am the Image of God; I am one with the Father—one in love, goodness and grace. I said, "He who has seen Me has seen the Father" (John 14:9). To know the Father more intimately, look at Me; I'm the *Image of the Invisible God.*

Jesus, I praise the Father in whose image You exist. One look at You satisfies my curiosity about God. You are the matchless beauty of deity. Amen.

Reading: Colossians 1:1-15

Key Thought: I show you how God would live and act in human flesh.

4
I Am Jesus: Worthy

I Am Jesus the Lord, receive glory and honor and power; for I created all things, and by My will they exist and were created.
—Revelation 4:11

They cried, worthy is the Lamb who was slain to receive power and riches and wisdom, and strength and honor and glory and blessing!
—Revelation 5:12

I am Jesus, *Worthy* to receive your worship for two extraordinary reasons: First, you should worship Me because I am the omnipotent Creator, "and without Me nothing was made that was made" (John 1:3). I have given you life, purpose and existence, because you were created in My image. Because of My creative act at the beginning of the world, all created beings—angels and redeemed souls—cry out praise and adoration to Me. Have you given Me praise and adoration on Earth?

Lord Jesus, I cry, "Holy, holy, holy," for Your awesome power that created me. You are Worthy to receive my praise for Your saving grace, which redeemed me.

I am Jesus, *Worthy* for another reason—My sacrificial death for all people and My specific pardon of your sin. I was not worthy of a cruel death, but still I chose to die for you. I had great glory and power in Heaven, but became *Worthy* of even more adoration because I purchased redemption on the Cross. John wept because he thought no one was *Worthy* to open and read the scroll, the title deed to Heaven and Earth. But I stepped forward to do it because I was qualified (See Revelation 5:4, 8-10). That makes Me *Worthy* of all praise in Heaven and Earth.

> *Lord Jesus, I fall down at Your feet to cry, "Worthy is the Lamb," because You created all things. You are Worthy to open the scroll because You redeemed me. Amen.*

Reading: Revelation 4

Key Thought: I Am Creator and Redeemer, I am *Worthy* of your praise.

5
I Am Jesus, the All and In All

Where there is neither Greek nor Jew, circumcised nor uncircumcised, barbarian, Scythian, slave nor free, but Christ is all and in all.

—Colossians 3:11

I am Jesus the All, and in All. When you become a member of My church—the Body—you are equal with all other believers. I indwell all believers, no matter who they are. I am ready to answer all prayers equally, no matter who prays. I protect, guide, bless, and use all believers, no matter their ethnic or economic background. All who are members of My body have equal rights, and to each I am the All, and in All. No one is lost or overlooked. You'll always have access to all that I want to give you. Will you claim it? You'll never be left behind, nor will I exalt anyone over another. You are special to Me and I love you eternally. I am all you would want, in all situations, at all times. Will you be satisfied with Me?

Lord Jesus, forgive me when I whine over things that don't matter and that aren't necessary. Help me see clearly Your care for me and help me experience deeply Your love.

I am Jesus who is all you have ever needed and when you trust Me, I will be all you'll ever want. To find satisfaction in life, look to the things that are important and forget about the things that are not important.

Jesus, You are the most important one in my life. Forgive me when I've given You second place. You are my All and in All. Teach me to look beyond people, things and places, so I can have satisfaction in You. Amen.

Reading: Psalm 149

Key Thoughts: I am Jesus the One who should be the most important Person in your life.

6
I Am Jesus, the Young Child

And when they had come into the house, they saw the young Child with Mary His mother, and fell down and worshiped Him. And when they had opened their treasures, they presented gifts to Him: gold, frankincense, and myrrh.
—Matthew 2:11

I Jesus was a Young Child when the wise men came to Bethlehem to worship Me with gifts and worship Me. The title "Young Child" means more than a baby in arms. I was an infant, crawling and even walking. This means there was a period of time between the shepherd's visit and the wise men's visit. It shouldn't surprise you that I grew as a Young Child (See Luke 2:40, 52). That's what children do. It shouldn't surprise you that the wise men of understanding and position would do. "They saw Me the young Child…and fell down and worshipped Him" (Matthew 2:11). Most people only cuddle young children or enjoy their antics; but they worshipped Me as God. You should respond the same way…worship.

Lord Jesus, I worship at Your feet because you are God. But I also worship at Your feet for what You did on the Cross.

The wise men worshiped Me the *Young Child* with gifts; "And when they opened their treasures, they presented gifts to Me: gold, frankincense, and myrrh"

(Matthew 2:11). Today, when you visit a newborn baby and family, you take a gift. You should do what the wise men did. Are you worshipping Me today?

Lord Jesus, I come to worship, giving You my time, my talent, and my treasure. But beyond these things, I give You my greatest gift; I give You myself. Amen.

Reading: Matthew 2:1-12

Key Thoughts: The greatest gift of all is giving yourself to Me, the *Young Child*.

7
I Am Jesus the Triumphant Lamb

And John looked, and behold, in the middle of the throne…stood a Lamb as though it had been slain.

—Revelation 5:6

I am Jesus the *Triumphant Lamb* who was slain to save you and give you victory. When no one else could open the Book of Life, My death gave Me authority to open the book. It was the title deed to heaven and earth. I stand in Heaven with seven crowns that symbolize My ruling power. I stand complete in My Father's plan. Because I am that *Triumphant Lamb*, I will complete the Father's purpose in the last day. But today, I can complete the Father's purpose in your life. The question is not why sin seems to be so triumphant today; the question is will you let Me defeat sin that you face?

O meek and tender Lamb of God, I come to You for forgiveness. Take away my sin. Give me victory!

I am Jesus the *Lamb* who stood silently before My accusers. "I was oppressed and I was afflicted, yet I opened not My mouth; I was led as a lamb to the slaughter" (Isaiah 53:7). I was the sacrificial Lamb that took away the sins of the world (See John 1:29). I understand your frailty and weakness; I can take away your sin because I took it upon Myself. I died for you. Now you will not die for your sin.

> *O Lamb, out of Your weakness comes strength; out of Your meekness comes honor. I sing a new song with those in Heaven, "Thou art worthy, O Lord, to receive glory and honor and power" (Revelation 4:11). I marvel at Your greatness and sing again, "Worthy is the Lamb who was slain to receive...wisdom, and strength...and blessings" (5:12). Amen.*

Reading: Revelation 5:13-6:1

Key Thought: I am Jesus the *Triumphant Lamb* who can give you victory.

8
I Am Jesus the Unspeakable Gift

Thanks be unto the Father for His unspeakable gift.

—2 Corinthians 9:15, KJV

I am Jesus the *Unspeakable Gift*. Receive Me as you would receive any gift. Remember, a gift is free; if you have to work for it, it's not a gift. You can't pay for a gift; you can't work for a gift, you put it on your credit card. All you can do is receive a gift. I am the *Unspeakable Gift of Salvation;* receive Me freely.

Jesus, I receive You into my heart. I am saved by grace through faith, not by works; salvation is Your gift to me (See Ephesians 2:8, 9). Your gift is greater than anything in life. Teach me to appreciate my salvation and to live accordingly.

I am Jesus the *Unspeakable Gift*. Words are not adequate to describe Me. I am greater than the human mind can conceive and more precious than the human heart desires. Human words can't adequately express the worth of My salvation. I am the *Unspeakable Gift,* greater than anything on Earth. Any fun you have in the world cannot compare to My joy. Any financial gain does not compare to My riches. Any good for which you strive cannot compare to the satisfaction of finding Me and making Me the center of your life. Thank the Father today for your *Unspeakable Gift* of me, your Savior.

Lord Jesus, my words are not adequate to express my feelings, so look within my heart to receive the worship that is there. And when my words of worship are not adequate, look deeper in my heart to discover my love for You. Amen.

Reading: Luke 19:1-27

Key Thought: I am Jesus, greater than anything you can describe.

9
I Am Jesus Savior

For there is born to you this day in the city of David a Savior, who is Christ the Lord.
—Luke 2:11

I am Jesus the *Savior,* the title that means "deliverer" or "preserver." I have many names, but the most important name may be "*Savior,*" because I am the only One who can save you. "Salvation is of the Lord" (Jonah 2:9). I am Jesus the *Savior* who will deliver you in many ways. I have saved you from the guilt of past sin and from the present bondage of sin, and I will save you from the future penalty of sin. When you die, I will take you to Heaven.

Jesus, You have done so many things for me—things I don't even realize. But Your most important gift was saving me; thank You. I feel confident in Your salvation, yet I want more. I want to enjoy all the benefits possible that come from salvation.

I am Jesus, the *Savior* (See 2 Peter 1:1). John referred to Me as "Savior of the world" (1 John 4:14). The Caesars of the Roman Empire who called themselves the saviors of the world, but they could only give military deliverance. I came to save you from damnation and eternal death. I will save you from weaknesses, temptations, attacks from Satan, and addiction to sin. I will save all those who come to Me.

I praise You Jesus, for "so great salvation" (Hebrews 2:3). You have saved me in so many ways; continue to save me to the very end. Amen.

Reading: Luke 2:8-20

Key Thought: I am Jesus who saves you completely in every way.

10
I Am Jesus Rabboni

I said to her, "Mary!" She turned and said to Me, "Rabboni!" (which is to say, Teacher).
—John 20:16

I am Jesus, *Rabboni*. The normal title for teacher was "Rabbi." My title *"Rabboni"* was not used by just anyone or any student; only those who had a special relationship to their rabbi used the title *"Rabboni."* Because I had cast demons out of Mary Magdalene, she called Me *Rabboni*. Because I had given sight to blind Bartimaeus, he too called Me *Rabboni* (See Mark 10:51). You should be grateful as Mary Magdalene, who called Me *Rabboni*. You should be grateful for the forgiveness of sin. You should be as grateful as Bartimaeus, who called Me *Rabboni* because he was grateful for the work I did in his life.

Jesus, You are my special Rabboni because You have forgiven my sins and revealed Yourself to me. Thank you for working in my life.

I am *Rabboni*. Not everyone can call Me by this unique title because not everyone has a saving relationship with Me. But because you believe in Me, you have a special relationship to Me. I become *Rabboni* to those who desire to know Me intimately (See Philippians 3:10). Paul said, "For to me, to live is Christ, and to die is gain" (1:21). If that's your passion, you can call Me *Rabboni*.

You are my Rabboni. I am grateful for the new life You gave me. You are the resurrected Christ, the One whom Mary saw on that first Easter morning. And like Mary, I call You Rabboni with deepest love and lasting commitment. Amen.

Reading: John 20:11-16

Key Thought: I am Jesus, *Rabboni* to those who have a special relationship to Me.

11
I Am Jesus the Carpenter's Son

Is this not the carpenter's son? Is not His mother called Mary? And His brothers James, Joses, Simon, and Judas?
—Matthew 13:55

I am Jesus, a *Carpenter's Son*. Joseph, My stepfather was My legal guardian. I was born of the Virgin Mary, but it was Joseph whose occupation provided Me food, clothing and shelter. Joseph was the human father who guided My growth and taught Me a trade. Since there is dignity in work, I became a carpenter, as was Joseph. When I was twelve years old, I went to the temple for My bar mitzvah, to be declared as "Son of the Law." It was then Joseph had to declare I would take up his trade. I worked as a carpenter in Nazareth until I was baptized by John the Baptist, at approximately 30 years of age (See Luke 3:23). I then began My earthly ministry. What can you learn from Me?

Jesus, thank You for submitting to the limitations of a human body. You gave me an example how to work for a living. Help me follow Your example.

Even though I was God, I became a *Carpenter's Son* to grow as you must grow, to learn as you must learn, and gain favor with man, as you must do. But don't forget that I left you an example of how you should work. Follow My example.

> *Jesus, I want to walk through life as You walked. I want to be successful at an occupation as You were. I want to learn obedience as You did (Hebrews 5:8). I want to please the heavenly Father as You did, help me today. Amen.*

Reading: Luke 2:40-52

Key Thought: I gave you an example of earthly work.

12
I Am the Lord Jesus Christ

This is Revelation of Me, Jesus Christ, which the Father gave Me to show our servants—things which must shortly take place.
—Revelation 1:1

My composite name is he *Lord* Jesus Christ. That's the name John called Me at the end of the first century when he wrote the book of Revelation. However, in the Gospels I am mostly called by My Greek name "Jesus," which reflects My earthly life. My name "Jesus" comes from "Joshua" in Hebrew, root meaning "Jehovah Saves." In the book of Acts, I am mostly called by My title, "Lord," which emphasized that I am the second Person of the Trinity and I was God. In the Epistles, I am mostly called by My office title, "Christ." Put them all together, and I am the *Lord Jesus Christ.*

I come to You as Savior, thanking You for salvation, but I worship before You as my God. I marvel at the depth of Your person that is reflected in Your many names and titles.

When My title "Lord" appears first in sequence, (the *Lord Jesus* Christ), it is emphasizing I am God. When My office title "Christ" appears first in sequence (Christ Jesus, the Lord) it is emphasizing My accomplishment on Calvary. When My name "Jesus" (Jesus Christ, the Lord) appears first, it is emphasizing

My earthly humanity. The book of Revelation is about Me; thus, it is called the Revelation of Jesus Christ. The emphasis is not on judgment, symbols, or Satan. It is the revelation of who I am and why I am returning to Earth. Study to see My many names in the first chapter of Revelation.

> *Jesus, reveal Yourself to me in the pages of Your Word. Help me understand You as I understand Your many names and titles. Amen.*

Read: Revelation 1

Key Thought: My names and titles reveal My nature.

13
I Am Jesus Rabbi

Then I turned, and seeing them following, said to them, "What do you seek?" They said to Me, "Rabbi" (which is to say, when translated, Teacher).

—John 1:38

I am Jesus, *Rabbi*. This title is a transliteration (the letters cross over into English, letter for letter) of the Aramaic word for "teacher." Just as you respect teachers for what they know and reveal to you, so revere Me as your *Rabbi*, because I am the revelation of the Father to the world. Those who saw Me, saw the Father (John 14:9). I instruct you about the Father and what He is like. I am your *Rabbi*.

Jesus, You are more than a spiritual teacher; You are the Son of God, the only One who can teach me salvation. Be my Rabbi; teach me all I need to know. Teach me how to walk in grace, and how to live for You.

A rabbi was also called master, because he was the master of his students. In other words, a Rabbi was a change agent in the life of his students. I am your *Rabbi*, not only because of what I know, but also because I am the Change Agent of your heart. I will help you know the Scriptures, and I will help you do the will of the Father. Just as there is an intimate relationship between a teacher and pupil, so your passion should be to know Me your Rabbi (See Philippians 3:10). I want to influence your life and be your Lord; will you let Me do it?

Rabbi, I will learn Your teachings, and let Your Scriptures control my life. Be the Master of my life. Guide me and direct me this day. Amen.

Reading: John 1:29-42

Key Thought: I am Jesus your Rabbi who will teach you what you need to know.

14
I Am Jesus the Precious One

Therefore, to you who believe, I Am precious.
—1 Peter 2:7

I am Jesus the *"Precious"* one. A diamond is called a precious stone. As the best diamond in the world cost you much to purchase, so I am *Precious*, because My death cost Me everything. "You were not redeemed with corruptible things such as silver and gold, but with My precious blood" (1 Peter 1:18, 19). As an item is precious because it is scarce or the only one of a kind, so I am *Precious* because I am the only Son of God—there is none other like Me. I am *Precious* because I am the only hope for the dying. Saints hang on to Me because I am your guarantee of life after death. No one else promises to be with you then.

> *Lord Jesus, I want to walk with You and talk with You. You are my Friend, my Guide, my Protector, and my God. I value my salvation; it is the most precious thing in my life. You are Precious to me.*

Just as some items are sentimental or have precious memories, I am *Precious* to you because you remember how I saved you. You remember how I have helped you so many times in your life. But I am also *Precious* as you contemplate spending eternity with Me.

Jesus, You are Precious to me; You are my Savior and Friend. I treasure You in my heart for saving me, for keeping me and for answering all my prayers. I look forward to spending eternity with You. Amen.

Reading: John 12:1-11

Key Thought: I Jesus am more valuable to you than the most precious thing in life.

15
I Am Jesus My Name Is Wonderful

For unto us a Child is born, unto us a Son is given; and the government will be upon His shoulder. And His name will be called Wonderful.
—Isaiah 9:6

I am Jesus called *Wonderful*, a noun in the Hebrew language that Isaiah used as My name. Throughout the Scriptures, the word "wonderful" is used to describe miracles; it's a word that suggests the supernatural. I am called *Wonderful*, because I Am the source of miracles; all supernatural expressions come from Me. I am called *Wonderful*, describing My mysterious or secretive attributes. I have all the divine attributes, both those seen and unseen. My name "*Wonderful*" expresses those things about Me that you don't know. My name "*Wonderful*" reflects My incomprehensible nature. I am so *Wonderful;* you have difficulty finding words to express it. I also have a name written that no man knows but the Trinity" (Rev. 19:12). Mine is a *Wonderful* name.

Jesus, I praise You for Your wonderful nature, and I stand in awe of the wonderful things You do for me. When I don't know what to say in prayer, I simply worship in Your wonderful presence.

I Jesus am called *Wonderful*, a name that separates Me from the common things of life. My name lifts Me into the glories of majestic deity. Also, My name "*Wonderful*" expresses My glory. I am God's glory, and I bring glory to the Godhead. My name "*Wonderful*" puts Me in a class all by Myself. Call Me *Wonderful*, the separated One, the distinguished One, the noble One, and the only One.

> *Jesus, I call You Wonderful because everything I know about You and I worship You for all the wonderful things You have done for me. Amen.*

Reading: Colossians 1:16-20

Key Thought: I am Jesus, too *Wonderful* for you to describe.

16
I Am Jesus, the Preeminent One

And I Am the head of the body, the church, who is the beginning, the firstborn from the dead, that in all things I may have the preeminence.
—Colossians 1:18

"Preeminence" means "first," and I want to have first place in your life. Put Me first in your thoughts, your choices, and your relationships. When you do everything I would have you do, I become preeminent in your life. "Preeminence" also means "the best in quality and character." When you let Me control your life, you give Me the *Preeminence* in all that you do. "Preeminence" also means "the highest." There is nothing higher in Heaven than Me, so lift up your prayer to Me. Give Me the *Preeminence* in your home. When I have My rightful place, I can lead you, protect you and cause you to grow.

Jesus, I pause to recognize Your greatness and give You first place in my life. I exalt You to your rightful place. Come, be preeminent in my life.

Today, I Jesus am not preeminent in the affairs of the nation. But in the end of the age, I will rule all ethnic peoples and nations. Also, I am not preeminent in the lives of many peoples, but one day, every tongue (including the unsaved) will confess Me, and every knee (including the God-haters) will bow to recognize My

Preeminence. Those who make Me preeminent on Earth will be rewarded by Me in Heaven.

> *My tongue confesses that You are Lord. My knee bows to your sovereign rule of my life. I make You preeminent in all I do. Amen.*

Reading: Luke 9:28-36

Key Thought: Make Jesus preeminent in your life.

17
I Am Jesus the Way

I said to him, "I am the way, the truth, and the life. No one comes to the Father except through Me."

—John 14:6

I am Jesus the *Way* to Heaven; there is no other way to get there. Will you follow Me today? Because I am Jesus the *Way*, I invited some fishermen, "Follow Me, and I will make you become fishers of men" (Mark 1:17). I invited Matthew, the tax collector, "Follow Me" (2:14). Because I am Jesus the *Way*, I still want people to follow Me today.

Jesus, I've always been independent. As a child I'd pull at my parent's hand to run ahead. When I got mad, I'd pout and refuse to keep up. But today, I submit my will to You. Teach me to follow You.

Just as I left My footprints on the sandy beach of Lake Galilee, today I want to leave My influence in every place in life. I will do it through you. Your are My "footprints" leaving an influence for Me in the places you walk? When you help another, I want them to realize I've been there. When you share the gospel with another, I want the listeners to realize I've been there. I am the *Way*; when you don't know where to walk or how to walk, look to Me for direction. My way on Earth was not always easy; neither will your way always be comfortable, but it's worth it. Let Me "walk" through your life. As you follow My way, leave your footprints in the lives of others.

Jesus, I'll follow You through ease or difficulty. I only ask that You go with me and help me. Amen.

Reading: Mark 1:16-20; 2:13-17

Key Thought: I am Jesus who ask you to follow Me.

18
I Am Jesus the True Vine

I am the true vine, and My Father is the vinedresser.

—John 15:1

I am Jesus the *True Vine*. In the Old Testament, Israel was called God's vine, but the nation was an unfaithful vine (See Isaiah 5:1-7). In contrast, I am the *True Vine*. Israel was disobedient to the Father, but I was true to the Father's mission for Me. I was truthful in character and speech. On the night before I was arrested, I said, "I am the true vine" (John 15:1). Just as a vine gives life and energy to its fruit, so I give eternal life to those who believe in Me. Just as a vine gives satisfying drink, so I give joy and contentment to those who follow Me. Just as a vine gives shade to the weary traveler, so I give shelter from the burning sun of opposition and trouble. What do you need from Me?

Lord Jesus, You are true. You have kept every promise concerning forgiveness, eternal life, happiness, and protection. You are The True Vine who keeps His word.

I said, "I am the vine, you are the branches" (John 15:5). Looking at a vine, you can't tell which is the original stem and which is a branch. This is what I meant when I said, "You in Me, and I in you" (John 14:20). You must stay connected to Me because "the branch cannot bear fruit of itself, unless it abides in the vine" (John 15:4).

Lord Jesus, You are the Vine; let Your energy flow through me. You are the Source of Life; let Your fruitfulness grow through me. You are the Vine; I am the branches. Amen.

Reading: Isaiah 5:1-7; John 15:1-7

Key Thought: You must be attached to Me, the vine, to get life and fruit.

19
I Am Jesus the Door Of The Sheep

Then I said to them again, "Most assuredly, I say to you, I am the door of the sheep."
—John 10:7

During My life time, I knew a sheepfold is an enclosure to keep sheep from wandering or getting lost. It usually had rock walls, and sometimes was enclosed with thick thorn bushes to keep out thieves or predators who would kill or steal sheep. A sheepfold usually didn't have a roof and it had only one door. The shepherd slept across the opening of the door to keep intruders out and the sheep in. Thus, the shepherd became the door of the sheep. Sometimes, several flocks were kept in the same sheepfold. In the morning, the shepherd would call "his own sheep by name" and would lead them out of the fold (John 10:3). Each shepherd has a different whistle, and the sheep knew their master's call. "When I bring out My own sheep, I go before them; and the sheep follow Me, for they know My voice" (v. 4). I am Jesus the Shepherd of the sheep, and I know you by name. do you recognize My voice when I call you?

Jesus, thank You for calling me and protecting me. I will follow where You lead.

When a shepherd becomes the door of the sheep, he puts his life on the line. The shepherd will fight to protect his sheep because each one is precious to him.

The key is relationship. I know, call, lead and protect My sheep. I want that kind of relationship with you.

> *Lord Jesus, I am Your sheep. Thank You for giving Your life for me. I want to go in and out of the sheepfold to "find pasture" (John 10:9). Amen.*

Reading: John 10:1-13

Key Thought: I Jesus the Shepherd want a protective relationship with you.

20
I Am Jesus the Bread of God

For the bread of God is He who comes down from heaven and gives life to the world.
—John 6:33

I am Jesus, the *Bread of God*. Just as bread gives you strength for your daily activities, so I give you mental and spiritual strength to live for Me. Just as bread is enjoyable to eat, so I am your joy and satisfaction in life. Just as we bread keeps you alive (without food you would die), so I keep you living. You eat My bread when you read and study the Word of God. You eat My bread when you think on Me and meditate on the Word of God (See Joshua 1:8, Luke 2:19). You eat My bread when you attend church and listen to My Word preached. And of course, you could never give out My bread to a hungry world unless you first eat it for yourself and experience My goodness.

Lord Jesus, You are the Bread of life. Just as I enjoy warm bread right from the oven, I look forward to more fellowship with You.

I am Jesus, the *Bread of God w*ho came down from Heaven. When you taste Me, you begin munching on the good things of God. "Oh, taste and see that I, the Lord, am good" (Psalm 34:8). I am satisfying Bread, healthful bread, life-giving bread, and resurrection bread. "Whoever eats of Me…has eternal life, and I will raise him up at the last day" (John 6:54).

Jesus, You are good bread. I will fellowship with You forever. Could I have some more bread now? Amen.

Reading: John 6:32-44

Key Thought: I am Jesus the *Bread of God* who gives life to the world.

21
I Am Jesus the Truth

I said to him, "I am the way, the truth, and the life. No one comes to the Father except through Me."

—John 14:6

I am Jesus the *Truth*; I cannot lie. I will always tell you what is right, I will not deceive you. When you read My Word, it will always give you an accurate record of the past, and it will give you an honest description of what people are like today. When My Word predicts the future, its predictions will come about. I said Scripture "is truth" (John 17:17). Whether you are referring to My words spoken on the earth, or My words written in Scripture; both are true. Because I am the *Truth*, I want you to be truthful.

Jesus, it's hard to be truthful because I have a deceitful heart that always wants to put me in the best light. Forgive my sins and help me always tell the truth.

Truth never contradicts itself; it is always consistent. What I said on Earth was always true. My words were always consistent with the rest of Scripture, and the Scripture is consistent within itself. "The Scripture cannot deny itself" (See 10:35. Because the Bible is consistent, you can trust its message. Because I am the *Truth*, you can believe in Me.

Jesus, I believe that everything You've said in the Bible is true, I have read the Scripture, because I believe it is powerful. The more I know about this Bible, the more I realize that it's Your truth. Amen.

Reading: John 8:13-36

Key Thought: I am Jesus who gives you truth.

22
I Am Jesus the Light

Then I spoke to them again, saying, "I am the light of the world. Those who follows Me shall not walk in darkness, but have the light of life."

—John 8:12

I am Jesus the *Light*. I can show you where to walk today. I was the *Light* that shined into your heart before you were saved so that you were convicted of your sin and repented. I was the *Light* that pointed you to salvation. Today, I'll be your *Light* to show you what to do as you walk through your many decisions. I am a bright shining *Light*. I can enlighten you through the Scriptures, but you must study them. I can help you see clearly as you pray, but you must intercede diligently. I can give you light to make better decisions, but you must make time for communion with Me.

Jesus, take away my spiritual blindness. Help me see what I must do today. Don't let me stumble or get lost. Shine light on my path.

I am Jesus the *Light* of salvation. You may stumble when you walk outside the perimeter of My light, so always take Me, your *Light,* with you. Let My light shine, giving you illumination when you don't know what to do. You can always have the guidance of *Light* when you take Me with you.

Jesus, help me make better choices; keep me from making mistakes. Be Light to help me understand my friends and associates. Shine on me when I walk through dark, threatening valleys. Thank You for the warmth of your Light. I feel comfortable in Your presence. Keep me from stumbling in the night. Keep me in the Light. Amen.

Reading: John 8:1-12

Key Thought: I Am Jesus, the *Light* to guide you.

23
I Am Jesus My Name Is Powerful

Whatever you do in word or deed, do all in the name of the Lord Jesus.
—Colossians 3:17

There's power in My name—*Jesus*. Remember that signs and wonders are done through My name, *Jesus* (See Acts 4:30). My name, *Jesus*, cleansed the lepers and opened the eyes of the blind, and I can do what you need done today. Don't forget I can get your prayers answered in My name, *Jesus*: "If you ask anything in My name, I will do it" (John 14:14).

Jesus, give me discipline to overcome my weaknesses, power to overcome opposition, and strength to overcome disappointments. Jesus, I claim the strength of Your name to rid my life of all evil lusts. By Your name, deliver me from the Evil One (See Matthew 6:13).

My name, *Jesus*, can fix broken lives and can heal sickness. A man had never walked, but My name made him strong (See Acts 3:16). My name, *Jesus*, can dispel evil powers. A girl was released from a demon when Paul said, "In the name of Jesus Christ come out" (See 16:18). My name, *Jesus*, can transform your life and ministry. So, minister today in My name. Remember, "Whatever you do in word or deed, do all in the name of the Lord

Jesus" (Colossians 3:17). What can My name, *Jesus*, do for you?

> *Jesus, Your name is sweet; it gives me joy. Jesus, Your name is comforting; it gives me assurance. Jesus, Your name is powerful; I claim Your strength to overcome barriers. Jesus, Your name is awesome; I worship Your name. Amen.*

Reading: Acts 4:1-12

Key Thought: My Name of Jesus is powerful.

24
My Name Jesus Is Above Every Name

Therefore My Father has highly exalted Me and given Me a name which is above every name.
—Philippians 2:9

My name, Jesus, is a *Name Above Every Name*. It is more excellent than that of Adam, the first man, because I am the Alpha and the Omega. My name is more excellent than that of Noah, who saved the world from the flood, because I will save the lost from fire in hell. My name is more excellent than that of Abraham, the friend of God, because I am God's Son. My name is more excellent than that of Moses, who delivered Israel from slavery in Egypt, because My name is powerful to deliver any from addictive slavery to sin. My name is more excellent than that of any judge who defeated Israel's enemies, because I defeated sin, lust, and the devil on the Cross. What do you want Me to do for you?

When I'm in trouble, I whisper your name, "Jesus." When I must break a habit or overcome an enemy, I say, "Jesus." When I need anything, I pray, "Jesus."

My name, Jesus, is greater than every Old Testament prophet, priest, or king, because I was the focus of their ministry. My name, Jesus, is greater than every apostle, including Paul, because I called them, empowered them, commissioned them, and used them. What I have done for these, I can do for you.

> *Jesus, Your name is sweet, for it saved me from sin. Your name is powerful, for it gives me strength and hope. Your name is above every name. Amen.*

Reading: Acts 5:22-42

Key Thought: My name, Jesus, is above every name on Earth.

25
I Am Jesus a More Excellent Name

Having become so much better than the angels, by My inheritance I have obtained a more excellent name.

—Hebrews 1:4

I Am Jesus, My name is *More Excellent* than the angels. I sent the angels as ministering spirits sent to help you as an heir of salvation (See Hebrews 1:14), but I, Jesus came to purchase your salvation. I have a *More Excellent Name* than Moses, who led Israel out of Egypt and gave the Israelites the Law (See 3:3). I Am Jesus who fulfilled the Law and died to take it out of the way (Colossians 2:13-15). I Am Jesus with a *More Excellent Name* than the high priest, who interceded for Israel (See Hebrews 4:14-16). I Jesus give you grace, for which earthly high priest prayed. I Am Jesus who has a *More Excellent Name* than Melchizedek, because I obtained a better salvation and a new covenant (See 7:22-24). Because of the excellence of My name, you can go to the Father though Me at any time. Will you pray to Him through Me right now?

Jesus, I love Your name. Your name calms my fears and guides me each day. Jesus, Your name saved me and Your name keeps me safe.

Because I Am Jesus, with a *More Excellent Name*, you can pray in My name (See John 14:13-14). Because

My name has power, you can break addiction and cast out demonic powers in My name (See Acts 16:18). Because My name sets prisoners free, you can have a powerful witness to the unsaved (See 10-14). One day, every knee will bow to recognize and worship My name (See Philippians 2:9-11). Will you do it now?

Jesus, I worship at the sound of Your name. You are worthy to receive all honor, praise, and thanksgiving. Amen.

Reading: Hebrews 1

Key Thought: My name is Jesus, the key to heaven's power.

26
I Am Jesus a Column of Smoke and Fire

I went before them by day in a column of smoke to lead the way, and by night in a column of fire to give them light.
—Exodus 13:21

I did not lead them by way of the land of the Philistines, although that was near [closer].
—Exodus 13:17

I am Jesus the *Column of Smoke* and the Column of fire that led Israel out of Egyptian bondage. I did not lead them the short way, directly from Egypt to the Promised Land. I led them the long way, through the desert where there was no water or food. I wanted them to learn to trust Me in the wilderness in spite of obstacles. In the same way, I will sometimes lead you the long way, which may seem to you the wrong way. Sometimes, I'll lead you where there seems to be no outward food or water, and where there are obstacles. I may be leading to see if you'll trust Me. However, there are no wrong ways when I lead; just long ways, with more time to teach you the lessons to make you strong.

Jesus, Israel murmured in the wilderness; help me not complain when I don't understand where You are leading me. Israel refused to acknowledge You, but I submit to Your leadership in my life.

I led Israel in both the daylight and at night; so look to Me so that you won't get lost. Stop when I stop and follow when I start. Follow Me in good days and bad; follow Me when you're hungry and when you're full. Where I guide, I will provide.

Jesus, I want to follow as close as possible to the light, I want Your personal presence to guide me. Amen.

Reading: Exodus 14:1-3; 15:22-26

Key Thought: Learn My purpose when I lead you through difficulties.

27
I Am Jesus the Son of Joseph

Philip found Nathanael and said to him, "We have found Him of whom Moses in the law, and also the prophets, wrote –Jesus of Nazareth, the son of Joseph."

—John 1:45

I am called the *Son of Joseph* because he was My earthly stepfather and legal guardian. Therefore you are technically right calling Me the *Son of Joseph*. I was conceived by the Holy Spirit in the Virgin Mary when Joseph was engaged to her. Joseph could have legally annulled the engagement, but when an angel explained My supernatural birth, he married Mary (See Matthew 1:18-25). Joseph endured the embarrassing rumors I had been conceived out of wedlock (See John 8:41). As an earthly father, Joseph protected Me, provided for Me, taught Me the trade of carpentry, and guided My youth into manhood.

Jesus, You are the Son of Joseph. You are the Son of God. I will follow You and worship You.

Philip told his friend that I was the *Son of Joseph* (John 1:45). Are you willing to tell others who I am? Because Philip was a faithful witness, his friend Nathaniel became one of My 12 disciples. When Nathaniel had questions about Me, Philip simply said, "Come and see" (v. 46). Tell your friends about Me. When they have questions, tell them to look at Me and I will answer their questions. When your friends see who I am, they will follow Me as you do.

> *Jesus I know You are human, born of a virgin, the Son of Joseph. But I also know You are the eternal Son of God. I will learn from You and tell my friends what I've learned. I will worship You and be transformed by Your presence. Amen.*

Reading: John 1:43-51

Key Thought: Tell others who I really am.

28
I Am Jesus Immanuel (God with Us)

They shall call His name Immanuel, which is translated, "God with us."
—Matthew 1:23

The angel told Joseph to name Me *Immanuel*, which means *"God with us."* When I was born, God visited humanity. I came to live with people and die for their sins. I am God, even though many did not recognize Me. Today, I am still *Immanuel*, even when people don't feel My presence. Because I am with you, you can get Me to help you face your problems. I am with you, even when you don't realize I'm near. However, you must call on *Immanuel* to get My help. I am *Immanuel*, which means I'll be there when you need Me.

Immanuel, there are many times I can't feel Your presence. I want to feel Your nearness. I pray about my problems, but they're still here. I know You're by me. Manifest Yourself; help me make it through my day.

Because I'm *Immanuel*, you can win when you let Me direct your efforts. First, I will give you hope when you feel like giving up. Then I will give you a courageous spirit to carry you through the rough spots. Next, I will show you what to do and guide your steps. Finally, I'll give you the tenacity to press on to victory. *Immanuel* is with you, but you must call on Me to get help.

Immanuel, I know You are with me. Help me feel Your guiding presence this day. Release Your indwelling power to do everything I'm supposed to do. I claim Your presence for victory today. Amen.

Reading: Matthew 8:1-18

Key Thought: I will be with you everywhere because I am God.

29
I Am Jesus the Great I Am

Then—when He said to them, "I am He,"—they drew back and fell to the ground.
—John 18:6

I am Jesus the *I Great AM*, the eternal all powerful Lord. Moses asked Me what was My name. I answered, "I AM WHO I AM…Thus you shall say to the children of Israel, 'I AM has sent me to you'" (Exodus 3:14). The name "Lord" comes from the Hebrew verb that means "to be"; it is first person, repeated twice. When you say "Lord," you are saying, "I AM I AM." I exist in Myself and by Myself.

Lord Jesus, You are the great I AM; You are without beginning, and without end. You exist by Yourself and of Yourself. You are the Lord.

I used metaphors to tell people what I am like. I said, "*I AM* the Bread," "the Light," "the Door," "the Good Shepherd," "the Resurrection," "the True Vine," and more. When I used these metaphors, I was saying more than that I was Bread that satisfied or the Way to Heaven. I was telling My listeners that I was the Lord who was revealed in the Old Testament. When the soldiers came to arrest Me in the Garden of Gethsemane, I asked them, "Whom are you seeking?" (John 18:4). They answered, "Jesus of Nazareth" (v. 5). When I replied in return, "I am He" (v. 6), I pulled aside My humanity, so My glorious deity came bursting out. The soldiers fell backward to the ground in response. How will you respond to My awesome glory?

Lord Jesus, I bow myself with face to the ground. You are the Lord God of glory. I worship You, the great I AM. Amen.

Reading: Exodus 3:1-15

Key Thought: I am the great *I AM* of the Old Testament.

30

I Am Jesus the Anointed of God

Then I will raise up for Myself a faithful priest who shall do according to what is in My heart and in My mind. I will build him a sure house, and he shall walk before My anointed forever.
—1 Samuel 2:35

The kings of the earth set themselves, and the rulers take counsel together, against the Lord and against His Anointed.
—Psalm 2:2

I am Jesus the *Anointed of God*. The word "anointed" comes from the same Hebrew word that means "Messiah." When I was born, the people of Israel were looking for a Messiah-Deliverer to drive their enemies into the sea. They longed for a Messiah to sit upon the throne of Israel and to rule them in peace and righteousness. But I didn't come the first time as a Soldier-Messiah for political deliverance. I came to rule their hearts and to give them principles by which they could experience inner peace and righteousness. Any sensible king would prefer to allow the inner compulsion of his subjects to rule them, rather than his using outward coercion. Let Me be your personal Messiah, and let Me be your personal Deliverer. Let Me anoint you this day for the task before you. Let Me rule your life.

Lord Jesus, anoint me with Your strength to live this day; deliver me from selfishness and temptations. Come sit upon the throne of my heart to rule my thoughts, feelings, and actions.

I am Jesus the *Anointed of God* who can anoint you with a fresh focus and renewed strength. I can anoint you with confidence and a renewed determination to live righteously. I can anoint you with My presence so that you can enjoy My peace. You can know Me more intimately this day; that's your key to personal deliverance.

Lord Jesus, I wait for Your anointing. Let the oil of Your presence flow into my life. Heal me when I hurt, renew me when I'm exhausted, strengthen me when I'm faint, and revive me when I've lost my vision. Amen.

Reading: Psalm 2:1-5

Key Thought: My anointing can enrich your life.

31
I Am Jesus the Chief Cornerstone

Therefore it is also contained in the Scripture, "Behold, I lay in Zion a chief cornerstone, elect, precious, and he who believes on Him will by no means be put to shame."
—1 Peter 2:6.

Jesus Christ Himself being the chief cornerstone.
—Ephesians 2:20.

I am Jesus the *Chief Cornerstone*, the Foundation to Christianity and the Church. I am the *Chief Cornerstone* for your life. Just as a foundation is laid at the corner of a building and the superstructure is built upon it, so I am the spiritual Foundation upon whom you must build your life. I will give you direction about how to live. Rest on Me; I can hold you up. I can give you a secure future. Don't worry; I can hold you steady in the storm. When pressures come, I am a firm Foundation, the *Chief Cornerstone*. Do you need stability in your life today?

Jesus, thank You for stability. I know I have weaknesses, and I know where I fail. Thank You for never changing, for never failing. I will rest on You today.

Just as a cornerstone shows where the building will be built, so I am the *Chief Cornerstone* who will show how to build your life. I have forgiven your sins, but the

Christian life is much more than salvation. You must live for Me and serve Me. You must build every part of your life on Me. I will show how you should live and grow. Are you building on My foundation?

Jesus, I need Your direction in my life. I try to follow You, but sometimes I get sidetracked in the details of life. Show me what to do today and what to say. I need help. Amen.

Reading: 1 Peter 2:1-10

Key Thought: I will give stability to your life.

32
I Am Jesus Your Lord

But there were also false prophets among the people, even as there will be false teachers among you, who will secretly bring in destructive heresies, even denying the Lord who bought them, and bring on themselves swift destruction.
—2 Peter 2:1

I am Jesus the *Lord* (*kurios*) who rules the hearts of those who willingly learn of Me. But I am also the *Lord* (*despotes*) who will force submission on those who reject and deny Me. There are people who claim to know Me but hold false beliefs about Me. I am the Lord (*kurios*) who gave them the freedom to believe, but I am also the *Lord* (*despotes*) who will punish those who reject the truth of Scripture. That's because they have chosen to reject Me. The Bible describes their rebellion: "They willingly are ignorant" (2 Peter 3:5, KJV). Today, you have the Scriptures; read its pages, learn of Me, obey its truth and know Me the Lord (*kurios*) intimately.

Jesus, I will open the pages of Scripture to learn its teachings. I will obey its truth, and I will submit to Your rule.

I will Jesus your Lord (*kurios*), and I will bless you because you have yielded to My rule. Pray for those who reject the truth, that their hearts will be turned to righteousness. To those who reject Me, I will be the *Lord* (*despotes*) to judge them in the final day. Those who reject My rule today will be forced to submit to My decisions and judgment in the future.

> *Jesus, I want to know doctrine as accurately as possible so that I'll have Your blessing. I want to know You as intimately as possible so that I can be as close as possible to the heart of God. Amen.*

Reading: 1 Peter 2

Key Thought: You must recognize My lordship.

33

I Am Jesus the Lamb

These will make war with the Lamb, and the Lamb will overcome them, for He is Lord of lords and King of kings; and those who are with Him are called, chosen, and faithful.
—Revelation 17:14

Lambs provided three basic contributions to Jewish life. Lambs provided wool for clothing and food to eat, and they were the primary animals that Jewish people sacrificed as a symbolic substitution for their sins. I was the ultimate Sacrifice, "the Lamb of God who takes away the sin of the world" (John 1:29). Lambs are gentle; they don't attack or hurt other animals, just as I, the *Lamb,* was gentle to all. Lambs have no natural defense, such as teeth or claws; every other animal was given some form of protection. But I was the defenseless *Lamb* who had no one to defend Me at My trials, nor any warrior to protect Me from crucifixion. Lambs are meek, just as I willingly submitted to death. I said, "If My kingdom were of this world, My servants would fight" (18:36).

Lord Jesus, You are the meek Lamb slain for me. You are my gentle Savior.

I Jesus, the meek *Lamb*, shall return a second time to destroy the evil works of Satan. In the book of Revelation, I am called *Lamb* 27 times to remind the readers that even though I am gentle, I will return to judge evil. I will condemn those who rejected My salvation. I am the defenseless *Lamb*, who will return to rule the world.

> *Lord Jesus, You are the Lamb who died for the world. You will return as the Lamb to judge the world. Amen.*

Reading: Revelation 7:9-17

Key Thought: I, the meek *Lamb*, shall return to judge the world.

34
I Am Jesus a Sacrifice to God

And walk in love, as Christ also has loved us and given Himself for us, an offering and a sacrifice to God for a sweet-smelling aroma.
—Ephesians 5:2

I am Jesus a *Sacrifice to God* for the sins of the world. When I sacrificed My life for the entire world, it was the greatest gift that could be given. I am the Son of the Father, but I sacrificed My position for you. I am the second Person of the Trinity, but I sacrificed My rights for you. I am the eternal Lord of the universe, but I sacrificed the riches of Heaven for you. Because I was a *Sacrifice to God* for you, I want you to sacrifice your life to Me. I want you to demonstrate your love for the Father, just as I demonstrated My love for you.

Jesus, You gave up the royal palaces of Heaven to be born in a stable. You gave up everything for me; I will not give You anything less than my heart.

I am Jesus a *Sacrifice to God* and a sweet-smelling Aroma that pleased the Father (See Ephesians 5:2). I have given you the example of sacrificial love when I said, "I lay down My life. No one takes it from Me" (John 10:17-18). I sacrificed Myself because I loved you; now I want you to walk in love. "A new commandment I give to you, that you love one another; as I have loved you" (13:34).

Jesus, my love for You is shallow in comparison to Your love for me. Forgive my weak love, and stir me to more sacrifices for You this day. Amen.

Reading: Ephesians 5:1-8

Key Thoughts: I sacrificed Myself for you because I loved you.

35
I Am Jesus Ruler

But you, Bethlehem Ephrathah, though you are little among the thousands of Judah, yet out of you shall come forth to Me the One to be Ruler in Israel, whose goings forth are from of old, from everlasting.

—Micah 5:2

I am Jesus the *Ruler* in Israel. As *Ruler,* I have ownership of Israel, which means that I have authority and control over the nation. In My first coming to Earth, "He came to his own [the Jews], and His own did not receive Him" (John 1:11). The leaders rejected Me, telling Pilate, "We have no king but Caesar!" (19:15). I had the biological right to be King, because of My birth. I had the divine right, because I was sent from Heaven. Because the Jews only wanted outward peace and outward prosperity, they rejected My offer of inner peace and inward blessing. They did not want Me ruling their hearts.

Lord Jesus, even though the Jewish leaders rejected You, I accept Your rule in my life. Even though many still reject Your authority over them, I seek Your rule of my heart. I accept Your authority and control.

I was Jesus born a *Ruler*, but I can't rule everyone unless I rule each one individually. And I can't rule individuals unless My authority starts within the heart of each one. I don't force outward conformity; I want each one to give joyful obedience from the heart. Since My kingdom is peace and righteousness, I give peace to those who willingly obey Me. I give power to live righteously to those who love Me. Will you let Me be your *Ruler* today?

> *Jesus, I choose You to be my Ruler; come give me power to live a righteous life. I serve You out of love; give me inner peace and assurance. Amen.*

Reading: Micah 4:1-5:4

Key Thought: I must first rule inwardly before I will rule outwardly.

36
I Am Jesus a Stone Cut Out of the Mountain

Inasmuch as you saw that the stone was cut out of the mountain without hands, and that it broke in pieces the iron, the bronze, the clay, the silver, and the gold—the great God has made known to the king what will come to pass after this. The dream is certain, and its interpretation is sure.

—Daniel 2:45

When King Nebuchadnezzar saw the great image in a dream, he saw four coming, world-ruling empires: Babylon, Media-Persia, Greece and Rome (See Daniel 2:31-45). In the end times, the Roman Empire will be revived briefly. Then a stone will be cut out of the mountain to smash the revived Roman world empire. I am the *Stone Cut Out of the Mountain* who will crush the kingdoms that oppose the Father; and then I will rule the earth. Where earthly things look discouraging and you think governments are out of control, remember that one day I will rule the earth. But for now, My influence is exercised through individuals as I rule the hearts of people. Let Me influence your world by ruling your heart.

Lord Jesus, may Your influence flow through me today. Help me feel Your presence, and help me experience Your power.

Until I return as a *Stone Cut Out of the Mountain*, I will not directly rule the world but will influence the world through secular rulers. The hearts of the rulers are in My Father's hands, and He influences them concerning His will (See Proverbs 21:1). Most of the rulers of government do not recognize My authority over them, but without Me they could do nothing. Pray for the rulers over you so that I can rule their lives and influence your nation for righteousness (See 1 Timothy 2:1-5). Your prayer for the rulers over you is your contribution to better government and a better life.

> *Lord Jesus, I pray for those who rule my nation; help them follow principles of righteousness and justice. Amen.*

Reading: Daniel 2

Key Thought: Now I rule through the hearts of people, but one day I will rule directly.

37
I Am Jesus a Man Approved By God

Ye men of Israel, hear these words; Jesus of Nazareth, a man approved of God among you by miracles and wonders and signs, which God did by him in the midst of you, as ye yourselves also know.

—Acts 2:22, KJV

I am Jesus, a *Man Approved by God*. I was born of a virgin without a sin nature. I lived a perfect life without committing sin (See 1 Peter 2:22). But that doesn't mean I didn't have difficulties; I was tempted in all points as you are (See Hebrews 4:15), yet I didn't give in to temptation. Just as a sacrificial lamb had to be perfect to offer for sin, so I lived a perfect life so that I could be a substitute for your sin. As the perfect Man, I was approved by God to take your punishment and guilt.

Lord Jesus, I know that You became flesh for me. Thank You for Your human perfection. I worship You and cry out with other worshipers, "You are worthy, O Lord, to receive glory and honor and power" (Revelation 4:11). Yes, I say, "Worthy is the Lamb" (5:12).

I Jesus was a *Man Approved by God*. Because God loved the world so much, He sent Me to redeem all people. Because I am both the eternal God and the perfect Man, I qualified to be the Sin Bearer for all. Because I died, was buried, and on the third day I arose from the dead, the Father attested to My work and accepted all who believed in Me (See John 20:31).

Lord Jesus, I bow before You, thanking You for salvation. You were the only One who could have redeemed the sinful race. You are the One who redeemed me. Amen.

Reading: Acts 2:22-36

Key Thought: The Father approved My human life.

38
I Am Jesus the Lord Strong and Mighty

Who is this King of glory? The Lord strong and mighty, the Lord mighty in battle.
—Psalm 24:8

I am Jesus the *Lord Strong and Mighty*. Come to Me when you're afraid and losing the battle. Lean on Me when you're weak. I know that the battle is fierce, because I was mocked, beaten, and finally crucified. I know how you feel in opposition, so come to Me for help. Let My wisdom guide you, and let My strength protect you. Don't give in to the Enemy, and don't give up. Draw energy from Me, for I am the *Lord Strong and Mighty*. What do you need from Me?

Lord Jesus, I feel comforted when You are near. I get energy from You each day to face my problems. I feel secure in Your presence. Come help me face my problems today.

The world expects Christians to be weak and soft. That's because they've only seen one side of My personality. They've only heard about My gentleness toward those who suffer and My mercy to forgive. But I have another side. I am the *Lord Strong and Mighty*. I will defeat the armies of Satan in the last battle. I will judge and condemn those who reject Me. So today, I will fight for you. When you are attacked, I will defend you. When the battle gets fierce, get close to Me. I am the *Lord Strong and Mighty* in battle; call on Me for help right now.

> *Lord Jesus, I will not let the Enemy scare me; nor will I be afraid in battle. I look to You to fight my battles. Amen.*

Reading: Psalm 7

Key Thought: Trust My strength in your battles.

39
I Am Jesus the Savior of the Body

For the husband is head of the wife, as also Christ is head of the church; and He is the Savior of the body.

—Ephesians 5:23

Salvation means that you are in Me and I am in you. At your conversion, I came into your heart to become a part of your life. At the same time, you were placed into My body (the universal Church). "You in Me, and I in you" (John 14:20). All those in Me are saved, because I am the *Savior of the Body*. If you are in Me, then you are saved. Have you invited Me into your life?

Jesus, I have asked You into my heart, and You saved me. Thank You for coming into my heart to become a part of my life. Also, I thank You for placing me into Your Body to be a part of Your life.

I am Jesus the *Savior of the Body*. When you were placed into Me, you were saved from your past penalty of sin and from your future punishment in Hell. And today, you are being saved from servitude to sin. I have a wonderful plan for each one in the Church. I want you to love Me, serve Me, and worship Me. Think about it. I have a great and wonderful purpose for your life.

Lord Jesus, thank You for a new, purposeful life. Because I am in You, I will try to do Your will today. Because You are in Me, give me strength to do Your purpose. I need Your power today. Amen.

Reading: Isaiah 53:8-12

Key Thought: You are in Me, and I am in you.

40
I Am Jesus a Merciful and Faithful High Priest

Therefore, in all things I had to be made like My brethren, that I might be a merciful and faithful High Priest in things pertaining to God, to make propitiation for the sins of the people.
—Hebrews 2:17

In order to forgive your sins, I was made flesh so that I could identify with you. The Bible says, "I had to be made like My brethren" (Hebrews 2:17), so that I could be a *Merciful and Faithful High Priest*. I didn't forgive your sins without feeling or empathy. If I had done that, salvation would be impersonal and antiseptic. But when I became human, I understood your temptations because I "was in all points tempted as you are, yet without sin" (4:15). Therefore, I feel for you. I am merciful, not vindictive or judgmental. Because I am a *Merciful High Priest*, you can come to Me for help.

Lord Jesus, I come to You for forgiveness. Thank You for understanding my weakness.

I did more than a human high priest did; I am faithful even when you are not faithful. Just as there are stories of priests in the Old Testament who were not faithful to their office, so the Scriptures describe Me as a faithful High Priest. I was human as you are, so I understood human weaknesses. Even though you may disappoint Me, I never once was a disappointment to Myself or to the Father. Because I am faithful, I am able to make propitiation (satisfaction) for your sins.

Lord Jesus, You have never disappointed me, even though I have disappointed You. Even in my weakness, You forgive my sins. I'm thankful for Your mercy and faithfulness. Amen.

Reading: Hebrews 2:17-18

Key Thought: I became flesh so that I could be a *Merciful and Faithful High Priest* for your sins.

41
I Am Jesus the One Who Has the Bride

He who has the bride is the bridegroom; but the friend of the bridegroom, who stands and hears him, rejoices greatly because of the bridegroom's voice.

—John 3:29

The Bride is the Church—born-again believers, those who have been saved. I am the Bridegroom; it is *I Who Has the Bride*. In our society, the man usually courts the woman, just as I am the One who seeks the lost. In your society, the man usually asks the marriage question, just as I call you to salvation. In your society, the man usually pays the price for the engagement ring, just as I am the One who paid the ultimate price for your redemption. The man usually takes the initiative, "just as Christ also loved the church and gave Myself for it" (Ephesians 5:25). Because I have done everything, it is *I Who Has the Bride*.

Jesus, when I hang on to You, it's good to know that You are hanging on to me. I know I belong to You.

Because the groom takes the initiative, the bride usually says yes. Have you said yes to Me? Because the groom first loves the bride, she usually follows his leadership. Have you followed Me? Because the groom protects his bride and seeks her welfare, the bride will go live with him. Have you let Me care and protect you? "For no one ever hated his own flesh, but nourishes and cherishes it, just as I love the church" (Ephesians 5:29-30).

Jesus, I look to You for all my needs. I will obey You, love You and live for You. Amen.

Reading: Ephesians 5:22-33

Key Thought: I am the Bridegroom who looks out for you, as well as for your needs.

42
I Am Jesus, the Holy One and Just

But you denied the Holy One and the Just, and asked for a murderer to be granted to you.
—Acts 3:14

The Jewish leaders rejected Me, the *Holy One and Just*. They accused Me of being a blasphemer of God and a traitor to the Father's nation. They called Me a liar, a winebibber and a hypocrite; and they said I did miracles by the power of Satan. But I am the holy One, the second Person of the Trinity, the Son of God. I am pure and separated from sin. I could do no sin, for I am God. When you sing three times, "Holy, holy, holy," you correctly repeat the word "holy" for each member of the Godhead. I am the holy One, just as the Father and Spirit are holy. Will you worship My holiness?

Lord Jesus, I testify You are holy. You are holy in Your nature, Your works, and Your dealings with all mankind.

I am Jesus the just One; I never did anything unjustly. I did not treat the Jews unjustly, even though they lied about Me. I did not treat My Roman executers unjustly, even though they nailed Me to a cross. Just as I treated everyone justly in My earthly life, so I will treat you justly in all areas of your life. You can trust Me, because My nature is just, I will always do the right thing.

Lord Jesus, I have trusted You for eternal life. Now I trust You to guide Me and help me live this day. Help me to be holy as You are holy. Help me treat all people justly, as You treat them. Amen.

Reading: Acts 3:1-16

Key Thought: Because I am holy and just, I will always treat you fairly.

43
My Name Jesus Is a Powerful Name

That believing you may have life in His name.
—John 20:31

The angel commanded, "Call His name JESUS, for He will save His people from their sins" (Matthew 1:21). My name "Jesus" originates from the Hebrew word *Yehoshua* (its shortened form is *Yeshua),* which means "Jehovah Saves." "Yehoshua" is also translated as "Joshua," the name of the general who conquered the Promised Land for Israel. Many Jews were looking for their Messiah to be a soldier—general who would drive the Romans out of their land. I came to give personal redemption, not political victory. I offered Myself as your Savior from sin, not your deliverer from military tyranny. Salvation was not in military triumph; it was inward—"You must be born again" (John 3:7).

> *Just as the fishermen left their nets to follow You, I surrender all to You. Because You told me to take up my cross daily to follow You.*

My name "Jesus" is a *Name for Salvation.* "There is no other name under heaven given among men by which you must be saved" (Acts 4:12). You are saved through faith in My name (See Ephesians 2:8). But you do not receive salvation by merely repeating My name verbally. No! My name stands for Me as a Person who came from the Father. My name stands for My death, which brings you forgiveness of sin. My name stands for My triumphant Resurrection, which gives you new life. My name saves you because "as many as received Me, to them the Father gave the right to become His children, even to those who believe in His name" (John 1:12).

Lord Jesus, I love Your name. I now ask You into my heart. Thank You for salvation. Amen.

Reading: Matthew 12:15-21

Key Thought: My name, Jesus, represents the power of My divine Person and My saving death.

44
I Am Jesus the Word

In the beginning was the Word, and the Word was with God, and the Word was God.
—John 1:1

I Jesus was called the *Word* because I expressed the true idea of the Father, just as a written word represents the ideas of an author. I was also called the *Word* because I am the One who communicated the Father's desires to the people, just as a written word communicates an author's intent. I am also the *Word* because I interpreted the Father to the world, just as a human author interprets a theme to readers. Words are symbols of meaning, and I am the symbol who showed the world what God the Father was like.

Jesus, show me what God the Father is like. I will study the Word of God to better understand Him and know what You expect of me.

I am the powerful *Word* who lived in the flesh. My spoken words were also powerful, for My words raised the dead, calmed storms, and comforted the hurting. My written *Word* is just as powerful as My spoken words. The written *Word* can save, heal, cast out demons, and become the basis for answered prayer (See Colossians 3:16, Hebrews 4:12). I elevated My words to a supernatural level when I said, "The words that I speak to you are spirit, and they are life" (John 6:63). Peter agreed with Me when he said, "You have the words of eternal life" (v. 68).

Jesus, I love Your Word, because You tell me about the Father. I love Your words because they are spirit and life. Amen.

Reading: John 1:1-14

Key Thought: I am the *Word,* who communicates the Father to you.

45

I Am Jesus the Author of Your Faith

Looking unto Jesus, the author and finisher of our faith, who for the joy that was set before Him endured the cross, despising the shame, and has sat down at the right hand of the throne of God.

—Hebrews 12:2

I am the *Author of Your Faith*. I not only am the beginning of the story, but I am also finished the manuscript. A book is usually good because an author put it all together. Just as an author sees a problem and scripts a solution, I saw the sin problem of humanity and scripted a solution. Just as an author develops the story line or plot, I saw what I had to do and developed a plan to save humanity. Just as an author chooses the right words to express his story, I am the Word who expressed the story of salvation in My life (See John 1:1). Just as an author develops characters or actors to live out the story, I became the central character of salvation. Not only am I the *Author of Your Faith,* but also I have finished your story. Most people say, "I could never write a book." In the same way, others say, "I could never hang on to salvation." But, it's not about your ability to finish, for I am the *Finisher of your faith*.

Lord Jesus, I am in You—the Author—so I know my salvation story will be completed.

I can finish your salvation story because I finished My own story. I went all the way to the cross, endured suffering, and took all the ridicule. Because I finished My task, I will help you finish yours.

Lord Jesus, I look to You for strength when I am weak. I look to You to carry me through to the end. Amen.

Reading: Matthew 27:15-34

Key Thought: Because I finished My task in providing salvation, I can see you through to the end.

46
I Am Jesus the One Who Comes Down from Heaven

For the bread of God is He who comes down from heaven and gives life to the world.
—John 6:33

I am Jesus *The One Who Will Come Down from Heaven.* I am the only person to ever have pre-existence. I lived in Heaven before I was born. "I came forth from the Father and have come into the world. Again, I leave the world and go to the Father" (John 16:28). What does that mean to you? Because I came from Heaven—the eternal City—I can give you heavenly life, eternal life. In addition, I know all about Heaven, because I lived there, so I can tell you how you will live in our future home. Also, I lived with the Father, so I can tell you about going to live with Him. Because I came from Heaven, I can give you a little bit of Heaven on Earth. I promised that I and the Father would come to live in those of you who love the Father and obey Him (See 14:23).

Lord Jesus, I worship You, the Eternal One. You live from eternity past to eternity future. I thank You for coming to Earth to show us the Father, and to die for our sins.

I am Jesus *the One Who Came Down from Heaven* to tell you there's life and glory beyond the grave. If I had not come, you'd live and die like the animals. You'd be without hope for this life and without hope of life after death.

> *Lord Jesus, thank You for giving me reason to live, and thank You for hope in the next life. Thank You for living in my life and giving me a little taste of Heaven on Earth. Amen.*

Reading: Revelation 22

Key Thought: I came from Heaven to give you the assurance of going there.

47
I Am Jesus the Fruit of Mary's Womb

Then she spoke out with a loud voice and said, "Blessed are you among women, and blessed is the fruit of your womb!"
—Luke 1:42

I am Jesus the *Fruit of Mary's Womb*. The Holy Spirit supernaturally conceived Me in the virgin Mary, and nine months later I was born in Bethlehem. I am eternal: "In the beginning was the Word, and the Word was with God, and the Word was God" (John 1:1). I "came forth from the Father" (John 16:28). While My spirit and personality came from Heaven, My physical body came from Mary. I can rightly be called the *Fruit of Mary's Womb*. When Mary watched Me grow, she saw her physical son developing. The Bible calls Me "her firstborn Son" (Matthew 1:25).

Lord Jesus, thank You for becoming flesh to live as a human being. Thank You for limiting Yourself to be like finite people so You could die for them.

I am Jesus the eternal God who became fully Man. I, the Man, was fully God. I was the God-Man, always fully God and always fully Man. While humans can't understand it, they read these apparent contradictions in the Bible and accept them both. They harmonize perfectly in Me. As a human, I felt tired, hungry and thirsty. I didn't know who touched Me (See Mark 5:31); and I didn't know the date of My second coming (See Matthew 24:36), though I knew I was coming back. As God, I raised the dead (See Mark 5:38-42), calmed a storm (See 6:47-51) and read people's thoughts (See 2:8). I am the wonderful *Fruit of Mary's Womb!*

> *Lord Jesus, thank You for coming to Earth to be born of Mary; I will try to follow Your example as a Man; I will worship You as God. Amen.*

Reading: Luke 1:36-45

Key Thought: I received My body from Mary through which I fulfilled My task on Earth.

48
I Am Jesus the One Who Sanctifies

For both He who sanctifies and those who are being sanctified are all of one, for which reason He is not ashamed to call them brethren.
—Hebrews 2:11

I am Jesus *the One Who Sanctifies* you. The word "sanctify" means "to set apart." You are set apart to God the Father and set apart from sin. The moment you get saved, I begin sanctifying you. I said, "You in Me, and I in you" (John 14:20). When you were saved, I entered your life; I indwell your life. But also, you were identified with Me; you are in Me. This happened so you might be sanctified, set apart from the world, the flesh and the Devil. I have already sanctified you in Heaven; now you must work it out in your daily life on Earth. You must set yourself apart from sin to live for Me.

Lord Jesus, I want to live a holy life, but it's hard. Help me! I want to experience Your presence daily, but I get distracted. Keep working Your sanctification in my life.

I began a good work in you at conversion, and I will continue to work in your heart (See Philippians 1:6). Listen to My voice, heed My guidance, and let My indwelling presence work itself out in your daily activities. You will not reach perfection in your earthly life, but you can grow toward perfection when you let Me strengthen all you do.

Lord Jesus, thank You for sanctifying me in Heaven. I want my earthly life to reflect my heavenly position. Work today in my life to make me like You. Amen.

Reading: Hebrews 2:5-12

Key Thought: You can grow to be like Me.

49
I Am Jesus the Babe

And this will be the sign to you: You will find a Babe wrapped in swaddling cloths, lying in a manger.

—Luke 2:12

I am Jesus the *Babe* born in Bethlehem, the One born to a virgin. I did not come in a spaceship, nor by some aberrant or bizarre entrance into the world. I existed throughout eternity past, but I "became flesh" (John 1:14) and came as a little baby into the world. I needed a mother to care and love Me, just as any other child did. I played with other children and learned lessons at Mary's knee. Because I was human, I know your problems. Will you talk to Me about your problems?

Lord Jesus, because You became human, You know how weak I am. I need strength to stand as a Christian in a non-Christian world. I need strength to keep on living for You.

I am Jesus the *Babe* who grew in "wisdom and stature, and in favor with God and men" (Luke 2:52). So, I know how you must grow both physically and spiritually. Because I was the *Babe* of Bethlehem, I can identify with your weaknesses and help you overcome them. "I learned obedience by the things which I suffered" (Hebrews 5:8); therefore, I can help you through your pain and problems. Look to Me for help.

Lord Jesus, I have never been spat upon for being a Christian; nor have I been beaten or nailed to a cross. But I face many hardships. Life is difficult; can You help me? I look to Your human example; I'm trusting Your inner strength. Amen.

Reading: Luke 2:1-20

Key Thought: I understand your problems, because I was human.

50
I Am Jesus a Star Out of Jacob

I see Him, but not now; I behold Him, but not near; a Star shall come out of Jacob; a Scepter shall rise out of Israel.

—Numbers 24:17

I am Jesus pictured as a *Star Out of Jacob*. Just as mariners plot their course by the stars, so I want to direct your life by the *Star Out of Jacob*. Just as stars give light in the black night, so I, the *Star out of Jacob*, give light to a world darkened by sin. Just as stars tell the time and seasons (See Genesis 1:14), so I give meaning to your appointment calendar. Just as stars warn people that they have a limited amount of time left on this earth, so I, the *Star out of Jacob*, give hope. Look to Me for meaning in your life.

Jesus, I look to You for direction this day. Guide me to make good choices and help me shine Your light to those about me.

Those who walk in darkness hurt themselves; they need Me, the *Star out of Jacob*, to show them the way. Those who are lost in the black night are cold and disoriented; they need *The Star out of Jacob* to point them to the warmth of the Father's love. *The Star out of Jacob* reminds people that the Father loves them and has a wonderful plan for their life. Carry My light to them (See John 8:12; Acts 2:1-4); I want to light the way of everyone coming into the world (See John 1:4).

Jesus, I want to be guided by Your star. Keep me warm near the fire and shine a reading lamp in my heart so that I can learn. Light my path, and help me walk in the light. Amen.

Reading: Numbers 24

Key Thought: I give light to help people find the right path.

51
I Am Jesus a Righteous Man

So when the centurion saw what had happened, he glorified God, saying, "Certainly this was a righteous Man!"
—Luke 23:47

I am Jesus a *Righteous Man*. That means I did right things in the right way. A righteous man is right in his desires and thoughts, in the things he does, and in the way he does things. The centurion present at My crucifixion knew that the trial and My execution were not fair. He saw the Jewish leaders first accuse Me of blaspheme and then, when Pilate wouldn't recognize that as a legal indictment, the charge was then changed to treason. The centurion heard Pilate say, "I find no fault in Jesus" (See Luke 23:4); yet the Jews crucified Me anyway. I forgave My executioners and then told the repentant thief, "Today you will be with Me in Paradise" (v. 43). When the centurion saw My integrity in the face of lies and dishonesty, he confessed, I was a "righteous Man" (v. 47).

Lord Jesus, I don't measure up to Your righteous standard. I don't always do the right things; forgive me.

When the Jewish leaders and the Roman establishment schemed against Me, Heaven came to My defense. The bright noonday turned to darkness. When the Father couldn't look on the unfolding tragedy, the heavens became dark. As I died, an earthquake rumbled over Jerusalem and the surrounding hills. The Father's Earth was protesting the despicable things done to Me, the Father's Son. When the centurion had seen it all, he cried, "This was a righteous man" (Luke 23:47). I am a *Righteous Man* because I was God incarnate in human flesh.

> *Lord Jesus, You always did the right things; I recognize You as a Righteous Man. I worship at Your feet. Amen.*

Reading: Luke 23:46-49

Key Thought: People recognized Me as a *Righteous Man* because I did all things right.

52
I Am Jesus a Refiner's Fire

But who can endure the day of His coming? And who can stand when He appears? For He is like a refiner's fire and like fullers' soap.
—Malachi 3:2

I am Jesus the *Refiner's Fire* to judge those who call themselves the Father's children. I will return to separate true believers from those who only call themselves Christians. In Malachi's day, silver ore was crushed into small granules and then ground into powder. Water was poured over the powder to wash away the dross. The remaining silverlike powder was melted in a crucible. The more heat—*Refiner's Fire*—that was added, the more lead dross came to the surface. By blowing hot air over the melted surface, lead dross was blown away, leaving pure silver. When I return, I will judge all to determine who are My true believers. My breath is the Word of God; it will blow away the dross.

Lord Jesus, I'm not perfect, but I believe in You with all my heart. I love You with all my heart, soul, and strength.

There is much ore that looks like silver, but it's not. In the same way, there are many who look like Christians, but are not. Some are crushed by persecutions and ground to powder by trials; even then, true believers are not always identified. The water of the

Word of God is poured over you in sermons and Bible readings, but even that doesn't single out true believers. Only the *Refiner's Fire* of judgment will identify those who truly belong to Me.

> *Lord Jesus, I know in my head that You exist. I know in my experience that I've asked You to come into my life. I know in my innate being that I'm Your child. Amen.*

Reading: Revelation 20:11-15

Key Thought: I will judge all those who call themselves Christians in order to determine who is real.

53
I Am Jesus a Ransom for Many

Even as the Son of man came not to be ministered unto, but to minister, and to give his life a ransom for many.
—Matthew 20:28, KJV

A ransom is the price paid to release someone who is captured or kidnapped. Satan tempted Eve to eat the fruit of the tree of the knowledge of good and evil; she gave it to Adam, and they both ate. In that act of disobedience, they were captured by Satan—both they and all their posterity. To release these captives, a price was paid. "You were not redeemed with corruptible things,…but with My precious blood, as of a lamb" (1 Peter 1:18, 19). I gave My life's blood to pay the ransom price; I was a *Ransom for Many*. I am "the Lamb of God who takes away the sin of the world" (John 1:29). While My blood was the price for everyone in the world, it only applied to those who believe in Me and receive Me as Savior. It was a *Ransom for Many,* but it only applies to those who received Me.

Jesus, I love You because You first loved me. I will serve You because You paid the ransom for me.

I am Jesus the perfect example of a servant who ministers to others. I did not think of Myself—I thought of others. But I did more than think of you, I came and took the initiative. I gave My time, My strength, and My life for your ransom.

> *Jesus, I will give my life for others because You have given Your life for me. I will think of others, give my time for others and take the initiative for others. Amen.*

Reading: Matthew 20:20-34

Key Thought: Give your life for others, as I gave My life for you.

54
I Am Jesus a Stronghold in the Day of Trouble

The Lord is good, a stronghold in the day of trouble; and He knows those who trust in Him.
—Nahum 1:7

Ever since Eve disobeyed the command of the Father, there has been trouble on Earth. There have been political troubles, financial troubles, family troubles, and inner troubles. Just as Eve didn't have the power to say no, so all people struggle with the power of self-discipline. Because you can't say no, you bring trouble upon yourself, just as Eve brought it upon herself and all her posterity. No one can escape trouble. "Man who is born of woman is of few days and full of trouble" (Job 14:1). But I know your trouble, so I promised to be a *Stronghold in the Day of Trouble.*

> *Lord Jesus, You know the troubles I face; help me. You know the future troubles that are coming—troubles I don't know about; prepare me.*

The reference in Nahum 1:7 to "the days of trouble" has a twofold application. It applies to the future day of My judgment. When you're in Me, I will be your *Stronghold* to protect you in the Day of Judgment. It also applies to all kinds of present-day troubles. I will protect you inwardly by giving you courage, patience, and hope.

I will help you outwardly when you follow the principles of Scripture. I will give you victory through prayer and My divine sovereign work. Don't worry about getting lost and not finding your way; I know where you are, and I'll come get you.

Lord Jesus, teach me how to solve troubles so I can have victory. Teach me how to live with troubles when I can't eliminate then. Amen.

Reading: Nahum 1:1-7

Key Thought: I will help you with your troubles.

55
I Am Jesus Your Strong Consolation

That by two immutable things, in which it is impossible for God to lie, we might have strong consolation.... this hope we have as an anchor of the soul,...which enters the Father's Presence behind the veil, where the forerunner has entered for us.

—Hebrews 6:18-20

I am your *Strong Consolation* to overcome doubts. Don't worry about your eternal destiny; I am your Hope. Doubts come from within the heart, because believers still have an old sin nature (See 1 John 1:8-10). So don't look within your heart when you have doubts, look to Me, the *Strong Consolation*. You can be sure of Heaven, because I am already there for you. Just as a boat is anchored in the harbor to keep from drifting out to sea with the tide, I, your Anchor, am already securely grounded in Heaven; I'll keep you from drifting. Just as a royal delegation will send a forerunner into a city so its citizens can prepare for the dignitaries, so I am your Forerunner who has gone to prepare Heaven for you. I will let them know you are coming. Your doubts will disappear when you look to Me, who is standing in Heaven waiting for you.

Lord Jesus, I have doubts when I rely on my ability to reason things out. But when I look to You, my doubts go away; then I know Heaven is sure.

When you have Me in your heart, I am your *Strong Consolation* to take away doubts. I am standing in Heaven waiting for you. So walk in this life with assurance, play with confidence, serve without any doubts, and lay hold of the Hope set before you.

Lord Jesus, I know intellectually about Heaven, but I also know You in my heart; so I know I am going to Heaven. You are my Strong Consolation, my Anchor, my Forerunner. Amen.

Reading: Hebrews 6:13-20

Key Thought: Looking to Me takes away doubts.

56
I Am Jesus the Salvation of God

For my eyes have seen Your salvation.
—Luke 2:30

All flesh shall see the salvation of God.
—Luke 3:6

I am Jesus called the *Salvation of God*, a title first given Me in Isaiah 52:10. Simeon, an old man waiting in the Temple for the Messiah, called Me—the baby—the *Salvation of God* (see Luke 2:30). When John the Baptist, preached in the wilderness, he called Me, the *Salvation of God* (see 3:6). Notice I "had come from the Father" (John 13:3); therefore, I bring salvation from God the Father to Earth.

Lord Jesus, I thank You for coming into this world with salvation from the Father. I thank You for bringing salvation to me.

I am Jesus the *Salvation of God* from your past sins. They cannot be charged against you. I am the *Salvation of God* from your present sins; so don't be an addict to sin nor let the power of sin keep you in bondage. I am the *Salvation of God* for your future sins. "The blood of Jesus Christ His Son cleanses us from all sin" (1 John 1:7). You must deal with all sin—past, present, and future—according to 1 John 1:9, which shows progression from confession to forgiveness to cleansing. And finally, I am the *Salvation of God* who will remove you from the presence of sin in eternity. There is coming a day when you'll live in Heaven, never to struggle with sin again.

> *Jesus, You are my Salvation of God. I claim You for total salvation in every area of my life. Save me now, and save me in the future. Amen.*

Reading: Luke 3:2-6

Key Thought: I come from God for your complete salvation.

57
I Am Jesus the Bearer of Sin

So Christ was offered once to bear the sins of many. To those who eagerly wait for Him He will appear a second time, apart from sin, for salvation.

—Hebrews 9:28

I carried the cross of Calvary until I was no longer physically able to do so. Another carried the cross to Calvary for Me. But there, I was nailed to the cross; there I bore the sins of the world. No one else was able to take My place as the *Bearer of Sin*. I had to do it alone—totally and until the end. I bore the sins of many until the sacrifice was accepted and redemption was complete. Then I cried, "It is finished!" (John 19:30). I have done it all for you; what will you do for Me?

Lord Jesus, since You died for me, I will live for You. My sacrifices are small compared to Your great sacrifice, but I will bear my sacrifice for You.

I didn't bear only part of your sin; I bore all of it. So you shouldn't walk in guilt nor live tentatively. Be a bold Christian, because there is no sin charged against you. I, the *Bearer of Sin,* bore your sin with love for others and you. I said of My executioners, "Father, forgive them" (Luke 23:34). Then, I took time to welcome the repentant thief to Paradise (v. 43). So rejoice when you suffer for Me, and "be concerned for others as you bear reproach for Me.

Lord Jesus, in appreciation for all You've done for me, I will live joyfully this day. I will not complain when things don't go my way, nor will I gripe over irritations. Any suffering is a privilege, considering how much You suffered for me. Amen.

Reading: Luke 23:46-49

Key Thought: Endure suffering, because I suffered for you.

58
I Am Jesus a Teacher Come from God

> [Nicodemus] *came to Jesus by night and said to Him, "Rabbi, we know that You are a teacher come from God; for no one can do these signs that You do unless God is with him."*
> —John 3:2

Nicodemus called Me a *Teacher Come from God* because he wanted to compliment Me. Nicodemus was the most outstanding teacher in this day. I—who spoke accurately—called Nicodemus "the Teacher of Israel" (John 3:10), the original Greek words I chose suggested that Nicodemus was the most outstanding teacher in Israel. In your terminology, it might be parallel to the title "Teacher of the Year." Yet, Nicodemus recognized that I was superior to him, because Nicodemus said I was a *Teacher Come from God*. What do you need to learn from Me

> *Jesus, teach me everything I need to know to be more godly and effective in service. I will become Your student.*

I was often called Teacher. Just as a teacher gives you information you don't know, I will teach you what you don't know about My Father. Just as a teacher helps solve problems and makes you more effective in life, I can lead you out of your troubles and make you effective in Christian service. Just as a teacher is a role model, so I personify the truth and lived a perfect live on Earth. Just as a teacher loves and helps students, I love you and will come to help you in your hour of need. I can meet your deepest need because I am a *Teacher Come from God*.

> *Jesus, there is so much I don't know; let me sit in Your classroom. I will listen to You and learn from You. Teach me what I need to know. Amen.*

Reading: Matthew 21:23-32

Key Thought: I can teach you what you need to know.

59
I Am Jesus a Sweet-Smelling Aroma

And walk in love, as Christ also has loved us and given Himself for us, an offering and a sacrifice to God for a sweet-smelling aroma.
—Ephesians 5:2

A sin offering in the Old Testament was a sweet-smelling aroma to the Father. It was not sweet just because it was pleasing to the smell, as a person is pleased with the aroma of a cooking steak. My Father was pleased because the sacrifice symbolized the repentant cry of a sinner. In death, I became that *Sweet-Smelling Aroma*. I made it possible for you to be saved. Just as the sweet-smelling aroma of the altar of incense in the Tabernacle symbolized the continued prayers going up to the Father, so My present-day priesthood is a symbol of My continual intercession to the Father for you. Is My sacrifice pleasing to you?

> *Jesus, thank You for Your sacrificial love for me. I have learned from Your example of love. I have experienced Your love firsthand, so I will walk in love.*

I am Jesus a *Sweet-Smelling Aroma*. My death pleased the Father (See Isaiah 53:10). Now I want you to please the Father by your godly living. Yield your heart to Me, and I will help you do it. I want you to please My Father by yielding your time, talent, and treasure in service. I will help you accomplish much in your service for the Kingdom. I want you to please My Father with your worship, because He seeks worshipers (See John 4:24). Magnify the Father and Me today with praise, exaltation, and thanksgiving. I will join you as a *Sweet-Smelling Aroma* of worship.

Jesus, because You are my Sweet-Smelling Aroma to the Father, I worship the Father through Your intercession. Amen.

Reading: Mark 15:42-16:1

Key Thought: I am your *Sweet-Smelling Aroma* to God.

60
I Am Jesus the Sun of Righteousness

> *But to you who fear My name, the Sun of Righteousness shall arise with healing in His wings; and you shall go out and grow fat like stall-fed calves.*
>
> —Malachi 4:2

My name *"Sun of Righteousness"* applies to My second coming. I am likened to the sun, which has two functions. The sun burns up things. But also, the sun's warmth gives life and healing. When I come a second time, My judgment will be "burning like an oven, and all the proud, yes, all who do wickedly…shall burn…up" (Malachi 4:1). I am like the sun; I sear and scorch in judgment. But I am also likened to the therapeutic sunlight, which relieves pain and dispels sickness. I am like the sunlight, but I can have opposite effects. When I come, will I deal with you in judgment or in healing fellowship?

> *Lord Jesus, I look to You for some therapeutic heat on my pain and troubles. In this life there are accidents and sicknesses; shine some healing on me.*

I am Jesus the *Sun of Righteousness*, I will return with healing for those martyrs who have died for their faith. I'll completely restore those whose bodies are eaten with cancer, or maimed in an accident. The blind will see, the lame will walk, and all sickness will be healed. I am the Righteous One, meaning I will do the right thing for you, and I will do it in the right way. I am the source of righteousness because I am the *Sun of Righteousness*.

Lord Jesus, one day You will make all things right. Until that day, give us a little warm therapy for the hurts of this life. Amen.

Reading: Malachi 4

Key Thought: I am the *Sun of Righteousness* who will heal your pains and diseases.

61
I Am Jesus the Seed of Abraham

Now to Abraham and his Seed were the promises made. He does not say, "And to seeds," as of many, but as of one, "And to your Seed," who is Christ.

—Galatians 3:16

I am Jesus the *Seed of Abraham*. My heavenly Father promised a son to Abraham who would "bless all the families of the earth" (Genesis 12:3). I was born the Messiah, the One who would take "away the sin of the world" (John 1:29) and bring in a Kingdom of righteousness (See Luke 1:33). Because Abraham believed the Father's promise, Isaac was born (See Genesis 15:6). Eventually, millions of Jews were born into the world; I was one of those Jews. By faith, Abraham knew that I the Messiah would come from his seed. "Abraham rejoiced to see My day" (John 8:56). But I didn't come to bring salvation just to the Jews; I came to bring salvation to all the world. I brought salvation to you.

Jesus, thank You for fulfilling prophecy. Thank You for coming to Earth as a Jew. Thank You for dying for my sins.

Because Abraham was a man of faith who believed the promises of the Father, he looked forward to My birth. But you too can be a person of faith. How? You must first look back on the history of Abraham to believe that the Father's promises apply to you. Then you must look back to My work on the cross and apply salvation to your life. Finally, by faith you must study the Scriptures and apply all its promises to your life.

Jesus, I believe what the Bible says about You. I trust my future to You. I know that You will guide my life and bless me this day. Amen.

Reading: Galatians 3:13-18

Key Thought: The Father promised a Messiah to Abraham, I was that promise.

62
I Am Jesus the Savior of the World

Then they said to the woman, "Now we believe, not because of what you said, for we have heard for ourselves and know that this is indeed the Christ, the Savior of the world."
—John 4:42

And we have seen and testify that the Father has sent the Son as Savior of the world.
—1 John 4:14

I am Jesus the *Savior of the World*. But I'm also the Savior of one—the individual. Notice how the circle begins large and gets smaller. I am the *Savior of the World* (See John 4:42); then I am the Savior of the Church (See Ephesians 5:23); and finally, I am your Savior (See 1 Timothy 2:3). I am the Savior of people, one at a time. I love all the people in the world, but then the scope narrows to you: I love you and died for you.

Jesus, thank You for personal attention and for personal salvation. Thank You for being my personal Savior.

Since I am the *Savior of the World*; I died for all—all who are alive now, all who were alive in the past and all who will live in the future. I am the Savior from the penalty of past sin; have you asked Me to forgive every past sin? I am also your Savior from the power of this evil world; have I delivered you? I will be your Savior from the presence of sin at the coming day with "the appearing of our Savior Jesus Christ" (2 Timothy 1:10). Are you ready to meet Me, your Savior?

> *Jesus, You are my Savior; thank You for saving me from past sins. I claim Your daily power to save me from daily sins. I look forward to Your personal coming to save me in the future from the presence of sin. Amen.*

Reading: Titus 3:1-8

Key Thought: I am the *Savior of the World,* and also your personal Savior.

63
I Am Jesus the Fountain of Life

For with You is the fountain of life; in Your light we see light.
—Psalm 36:9

When you've been on a long hot walk, what you want is water. Sometimes the heat gets to be too much, and you're in danger of a heat stroke. You need some cool water on your tongue and something wet on the back of your neck. If you're in really bad condition, you stick your whole head in the water. When you need water to keep from fainting, I am your *Fountain of Life* who will give you a new presence of mind and a new focus. Do you need to cool down your anger, frustration, or bitterness?

Lord Jesus, I need some cool water before I leave home, because it's pretty hot out there. And, when I get home at the end of the day, I'll need more water to refresh my life for the evening duties.

Sometimes at work you need a drink of water to refresh your work habits. Sometimes you need a drink of water in the middle of the night because you wake up and your mouth is dry and you can't sleep. Sometimes a drink of water makes you think well, play better, talk better, or perform better. For whatever you need, pause to drink of Me. Just as water energizes the body, so My renewed presence will revitalize your life. Remember, I am the *Fountain of Life,* who called Myself "a fountain of water springing up into everlasting life" (John 4:14).

Jesus, I come to drink of You. Ah, water is good when I am thirsty. I'll keep coming back, because I need You daily. Amen.

Reading: Psalm 36

Key Thought: I am a *Fountain* of water to refresh your life.

64
I Am Jesus the Forerunner

Where the forerunner has entered for us, even Jesus, having become High Priest forever according to the order of Melchizedek.
—Hebrews 6:20

I am Jesus, the *Forerunner* who has gone to Heaven first for you. Just as a delegation used to send a runner ahead of them to a city to announce their arrival, so I too am the *Forerunner* who went into Heaven to announce the coming of the Church. I am your Forerunner who has announced your coming to Heaven. Just as a forerunner allows the people of a city to get ready for a delegation, so I am your *Forerunner* allows all of Heaven to prepare for your arrival. The Father has prepared a mansion for you (See John 14:1-3), and I am interceding to the Father for you. The angels are waiting for you. Everything is ready because I am the *Forerunner* who prepared the way.

Lord Jesus, I face death with more confidence, knowing that You've gone before me to Heaven. My doubts fade when I realize You're

waiting for me. I don't want to die, but at least I can look beyond death to see You waiting for me.

Not only have I gone as the *Forerunner* to prepare Heaven, but I also am now your Intercessor who stands at the right hand of the Father, interceding for you to overcome temptation and to make the trip triumphantly. So live confidently this day, because I am preparing Heaven for you. I am praying for you as you journey homeward.

Lord Jesus, I know You stand at the right hand of the Father, making intercession for me. Because You are in Heaven, I pray confidently and I live with assurance. Amen.

Reading: Hebrews 6

Key Thought: I am preparing Heaven for you.

65
I Am Jesus the Firstborn

But when He again brings the firstborn into the world, He says: "Let all the angels of God worship Him."

—Hebrews 1:6

I am Jesus, the *Firstborn* child of Mary; she had no children before Me. She was a virgin when I was conceived in her of the Holy Spirit. She had not known a man (See Luke 1:34). It was the Father's plan for Me to be her *Firstborn,* because most mothers give more love and care to their first child. Because of this care, I "the Child grew and became strong in spirit, filled with wisdom; and the grace of God was upon Me" (v. 2:40). I was the God-man, perfect to be your Savior.

Lord Jesus, I praise You for Your birth and Your growth to full manhood. Just as the angels in Heaven worship You as the God-Man, so do I.

I am Jesus, also the *Firstborn* of every creature (See Colossians 1:15), which means I gave life to everything in the world. I am "the Beginning of the creation of God" (Revelation 3:14). Not only was I the source of physical life, but I am also "the firstborn from the dead" (Colossians 1:18), the first one to rise from the dead. Now I am the source of all your spiritual life. Because you're in Me, you have resurrection life

(See Galatians 2:20). Because I am the *Firstborn*, I give you a hope of future Heaven.

> *Lord Jesus, thank You for being the Firstborn of the virgin Mary—to live and die on the cross for me. Thank You for being the Firstborn from the dead—to give me resurrection life. Thank You for the hope of future resurrection and Heaven. Amen.*

Reading: Hebrews 1:1-9; Colossians 1:13-19

Key Thought: I am the *Firstborn* of the resurrection—to give you life.

66
I Am Jesus Undefiled

For such a High Priest was fitting for us, who is holy, harmless, undefiled, separate from sinners, and has become higher than the heavens.
—Hebrews 7:26

I am Jesus the perfect Son of God. Just as the sacrificial lamb had to be without blemish, so I am the *Undefiled,* sinless Substitute who died for your sin. Satan tempted Me to sin, but I rejected the enemy's temptation (See Matthew 4:1-11). So I can help you overcome your temptation or bad habits. Some Jewish people accused Me of sin; but when I challenged them to name one sin, they were not able to do it (See John 8:46). In the same way, you should have a blameless reputation before your enemies. On the night before I died, I didn't want to drink the cup of punishment, but I drank it willingly, submitting to the suffering of the Cross (See Matthew 26:39-42). Just as I was perfectly obedient to the Father, will you willingly become obedient My will?

Lord Jesus, You are my example for godly living; give me the power to resist sin. You are my High Priest, who prays for me in Heaven; intercede to the Father for me.

"Undefiled" means "the absence of sin." But I am more than One who never sinned; I have all the positive attributes of holiness. I am as holy as the Father, so I can be your perfect High Priest.

Lord Jesus, I know You are my perfect High Priest, so I come asking You to help me in my struggles. Keep me from sin, make me holy, and use me this day. Amen.

Reading: Hebrews 10:26-39

Key Thought: I can be your Intercessor because I am *Undefiled.*

67
I Am Jesus the Son of God

*But these are written that you may believe that
Jesus is the Christ, the Son of God, and that
believing you may have life in His name.*
—John 20:31

I am Jesus the *Son of God,* the Second Person of the Godhead. My description "Son" does not mean I am less than the Father. We are co-equal and co-eternal, and We share these attributes equally with the Holy Spirit. The phrase "*Son of God*" means that I have the same nature as the Father, and that I am the personification of all the character-qualities of deity, I am Jesus, Son of God. Can you trust Me?

Jesus, I know that You are God, for only God can forgive my sins and transform my life. But, I am concerned when the world doubts who You are.

People have always doubted My deity. Even a man on a cross mocked My claims of deity: "If You are the Son of God, come down from the cross" (Matthew 27:40). But I didn't respond to doubting criticism in the way that the world wanted. I showed My deity by performing miracles of compassion and by forgiving sin. The Holy Spirit will work in human hearts to show them who I am (See John 16:7-15). The Father expects people to respond to My love.. I expect people to respond to My invitation to be saved. I am the *Son of God*, Creator and Lord, and in the final day, I'll be your Judge.

> *Jesus, I bow at Your feet, recognizing You as God. You are the Lord of the ages. I recognize you as my Lord this day. I worship You as the Son of God. Amen.*

Reading: John 20:24-31

Key Thought: You must recognize I am the *Son of God*.

68
I Am Jesus Son of the Father

Grace, mercy, and peace will be with you from God the Father and from the Lord Jesus Christ, the Son of the Father, in truth and love.
—2 John 3

I am Jesus *Son of the Father*. I was sent by My Father to save a sinful world. I am the constant object of My Father's love (See John 5:20). The Father and I are one in nature (See 10:30), but We are separate Persons. We talk to each other, love each other and work together to save the world.

O Son of God, I magnify You for Your power and love. I know You can do all things, so work in my life today.

I, the *Son of the Father*, want you to know Me and honor Me, as I honor the Father. Those who do not honor Me offend the Father (See John 5:23). Just as the Father raised the dead, so I give spiritual life to those who believe in Me (See v. 21). Those who are spiritually dead in sin can have eternal life through My words (See v. 24). Believers who have physically died will be raised to resurrection life in the future through My words (See vv. 25, 28). The Father has given Me the power to give life to all who believe and He has given Me the authority to judge sinners at the end of the age (See v. 27).

Jesus, I want Your power in my life today. I want Your words to give me strength and optimism to meet the challenges I face. I want Your indwelling presence to encourage me for all I do. Amen.

Reading: John

Key Thought: I, the *Son of God*, can give energy to your Christian life.

69
I Am Jesus Son of the Living God

Simon Peter answered and said, "You are the Christ, the Son of the living God."
—Matthew 16:16

I am Jesus *Son of the Living God*. All false gods have no life in them. False gods don't think or love; nor do they answer the prayers offered to them. They may be carved from wood or stone; they can't communicate with you, and they can't give life to those who worship them. I am the *Son of the Living God*; both I and the Father are alive and have always lived. There was never a time when the living God didn't exist. Perhaps the greatest creative act was when We breathed into Adam's nostrils the breath of life. And in that creative act, life was given to Adam; and through generations of procreation, life was given to you.

I come to You, Jesus, the living God, thanking You for creating me in Your image. Because I have a mind, I think about You. Because I have emotions, I love You. Because I have a will, I choose to follow You.

I am Jesus *Son of the Living God;* I gave you spiritual life through My death, burial and resurrection: "I have come that they may have life, and that they may have it more abundantly" (John 10:10). You have two kinds of life: (1) You received eternal life by believing in Me, and (2) you can enjoy satisfying life more abundantly by magnifying Me in all you do.

> *I cling to You, Son of the Living God, for without You I don't have life. But with You in my heart, I have eternal life. Today, help me enjoy Your abundant life. Amen.*

Reading: Matthew 16:13-16

Key Thought: I give you all types of life.

70
I Am Jesus the Son Who Is Consecrated for Evermore

For the law maketh men high priests which have infirmity; but the word of the oath, which was since the law, maketh the Son, who is consecrated for evermore.
—Hebrews 7:28

As an Intercessor, I don't need to be consecrated every day, as the Old Testament priests had to sacrifice daily for their sins. They had to be consecrated time and again because they sinned. It was impossible for them to enter the Father's presence unless they were cleansed each time they prayed. I am the *Son Who Is Consecrated For Evermore*. I am eternally consecrated—prepared—to continually enter the Father's presence for you. I am perfect—without sin—so I could be your Sin Bearer. So now I am the constant Intercessor for your sins. All day and every day, I stand ready to intercede to the Father for you.

Jesus, I constantly need You to intercede for me, because I constantly fail. I sin innocently; intercede to the Father for me. I give into temptation; pray to strengthen me.

I have an "unchangeable priesthood" (Hebrews 7:24). No matter what sin you commit, and no matter why you sin, I will intercede to the Father for you. Remember, "The blood of Jesus Christ His Son cleanses us from all sin" (1 John 1:7). Did you see that word "all"? I cleanse you totally from sin; so confess it, repent, and ask Me to forgive it. Then seek My power to overcome it. I want to give you victory. I stand in the Father's presence for you.

Jesus, I am amazed at Your grace and forgiveness. Thank You for cleansing my sin. Now make continued intercession for me. Amen.

Reading: Mark 14:32-42

Key Thought: I make constant intercession for your sin.

71
I Am Jesus the Resurrection

Jesus said to her, "I am the resurrection and the life. He who believes in Me, though he may die, he shall live."

—John 11:25

I am your *Resurrection*, which means that I gave new life to you when you were saved. You can know that I gave you this eternal life when I came out of the grave, because I said, "I am the resurrection." Now you are raised in Me; you will live forever. Your old body may die at your death (if the rapture doesn't come first), but your soul goes to live with the Father. At the rapture, your soul will be rejoined to your new glorious body. One day you'll have a new body like Mine.

Jesus, I believe in Your resurrection, thank You for saving me. Thank You for the promise of raising me in the future.

When I died, your sin died with Me. When I arose from the dead, you were in Me, rising from the dead. I am the *Resurrection*. Now you are in Me, and I am in you" (See John 14:20). You are seated in the heavenlies (See Ephesians 2:6). So let your life on Earth reflect your new heavenly position. Because I am the *Resurrection*, My life-giving power can indwell you and give you new desires to live godly. Because I am the *Resurrection*, you can be strengthened in your inner person by My indwelling presence (See Ephesians 3:16). Because of My *Resurrection*, I can give you spiritual victory today.

> *Jesus, I marvel at Your resurrection, and worship You for what you've done for me. I claim Your resurrection power to strengthen me to live for You. Help me overcome my problems and be victorious today. Amen.*

Reading: John 11:1-44

Key Thought: You can be victorious because of My resurrection.

72
I Am Jesus the Testimony of God

And I, brethren, when I came to you, did not come with excellence of speech or of wisdom declaring to you the testimony of God. For I determined not to know anything among you except Jesus Christ and Him crucified.
—1 Corinthians 2:1, 2

I am Jesus the *Testimony of God* to the world. Do not look for deep truths elsewhere; I am the Personification of truth. Do not look for mysterious wisdom; I am the Wisdom of God. Do not look for sparkling speeches or cleverly written words; I am the *Testimony of God.* You'll not find anything deeper in understanding than Me, nor will you find anything simpler to understand than Me. Everything that the Father wants you to know, you'll find in Me.

Jesus, I learn of You in the pages of Scripture. There is no grace greater than Your grace; there is no love greater than Your love. You walked humbly among men to show us what God was like; now I bow at Your feet to exalt You in my life.

I am Jesus the *Testimony* that the Father would have you know. Do not search for deep wisdom apart from Me. Do not seek to understand spiritual things that are complicated or confusing apart from Me. If you think you've found truth and I am not there, you are lost in the jungle of error. The Father has testified what you need to know. You'll find the answers to your questions in Me for I am the *Testimony of God*.

> *When I look into the crystal waters of a pond, I see the calm surface of a pool. Yet, the water beneath the surface is deep, so deep I'll never reach the bottom. Jesus You are like that pond. You are easy to understand, yet so deep that I'll never completely comprehend all You are and do. Amen.*

Reading: 1 Corinthians 2:1-5

Key Thought: I have told you what the Father wants you to know.

73
I Am Jesus the Triumphant Son of Man

Then I turned to see the voice that spoke with me. And having turned I saw...One like the Son of Man, clothed with a garment down to the feet and girded about the chest with a golden band.
—Revelation 1:12, 13

I am Jesus the *Triumphant Son of Man* who stood glorified and transfigured before John on the Isle of Patmos. My hair was "as white as snow" (Revelation 1:14), a symbol of My purity. My eyes were "like a flame of fire" (v. 14), symbol of My ability to accurately discern the nature of people. My feet, which were "as if refined in a furnace" (v. 15), were quick to burn away impurities and sin. I want you to be pure and truthful in all you do.

Lord Jesus, I bow before Your majesty; forgive my sin. Receive honor and glory from my life. Guide me to do things that will bring praise to You today.

I am Jesus the *Triumphant Son of Man* who stood before John in priestly garments. My voice was compared to "the voice of many waters" (Revelation 1:15), emphasizing My authority. "Out of His mouth went a sharp two-edged sword" (v. 16), symbolizing the Word of God that gives life. The brilliance about My countenance was "like the sun shining in its strength" (v.

16), reflecting My glory and transforming power. I the *Triumphant Son of Man* can transform your life. I can help you triumph over all your spiritual problems.

> *Lord Jesus, when John saw You, he fell at Your feet. I follow his example to worship at Your feet. As glorified Son of God in my life, I praise You for becoming all things for me. Help me see perfectly Your glory so that I can reflect it to the world. Amen.*

Reading: Matthew 17:1-13

Key Thought: Let Me the *Triumphant Son of Man* make you victorious.

74
I Am Jesus the Trustworthy Witness

And from Jesus Christ, the faithful and trustworthy witness.
—Revelation 1:5 AMP

I am Jesus the *Trustworthy Witness*; I came to witness the message of the Father. You can trust Me, for I perfectly witnessed to the world what the Father wanted said in the past. When I identified Myself as one with the Father, the Jewish religious leaders "sought all the more to kill Him, because He not only broke the Sabbath, but also said that God was His Father, making Himself equal with God" (John 5:18). I did what I was trusted to do, and I said what needed to be said. I am a *Trustworthy Witness* in the face of death.

Lord Jesus, thank You for faithfully witnessing about the Father while on earth. Thank You for faithfully witnessing to me about the love of the Father for me.

Remember that the word "witness" is translated from the Greek word for martyr. Those who are killed for their faithful witness are called martyrs. The religious leaders accused Me of blasphemy because I faithfully witnessed to them about the Father. I was killed for My witness. Now I want you to be a faithful witness for Me to the world, "You shall be witnesses to Me" (Acts 1:8). How will you witness for Me today?

Lord Jesus, because You died for me, the least I can do is be a trustworthy witness for You. Help me be worthy of the trust you placed in me. I will faithfully tell others what You have done for me. You can trust me to be a witness of You and the Father who sent You. Amen.

Reading: John 7:40-53

Key Thought: I want you to be a trustworthy witness for Me.

75
I Am Jesus Faithful and True

Now I saw heaven opened, and behold, a white horse. And He who sat on him was called Faithful and True, and in righteousness He judges and makes war.

—Revelation 19:11

I am Jesus called *Faithful and True*. These descriptions were not given to Me until the end of the book of Revelation. When John saw My second coming in power, he called Me *Faithful and True*. This compound name reflects My character. I am faithful to do all I promised, and I promised, "I will come again" (John 14:2). I am true and consistent to all that is established in the universe. My second coming is the appropriate climax to all I did since creation. I will be *Faithful and True* throughout the great tribulation in Revelation, so I'll be *Faithful and True* in your hour of trial. Right to the end, I'll be the same, regardless of circumstances, regardless of pressures, regardless of others' disappointments; I will prove Myself to be *Faithful and True*.

Lord Jesus, how long will my troubles last? The Evil One is strong and it's been so long. It's easy to get my eyes on tribulation and not on You. Help me look beyond my problem to see Your victorious triumph. How long?

I will always be *Faithful and True* to the plan I established when I created all things. I will allow sin to run its course, and I will allow the Evil One to do his work. But then I'll return, just as I promised, to judge sin and evildoers and to reward those who obey Me.

Lord, thank You for Your faithfulness to keep Your word and for being truthful about the reality of sin. Because I have trusted You for salvation, I will continue to trust You today. Amen.

Reading: Revelation 19:11-15

Key Thought: I will be *Faithful and True* to the end.

76
I Am Jesus the Only Wise God

Now to the King eternal, immortal, invisible, to God who alone is wise, be honor and glory forever and ever. Amen.
—1 Timothy 1:17

I am Jesus the *Only Wise God*; idols can't speak and leaders of false religions don't know anything. But because I, the Lord Jesus created people, I know what people think; I even know their motives and desires. I know everything about all people, so I know all about you. I know your temptations and your strengths. I know your spiritual dreams and your secret sins. I know what is best for you for this day. Will you let Me, the *Only Wise God*, guide you?

Lord Jesus, You know everything about me. You know I am not as strong as I want to be. Stand by me and help me today. You know what is best for this day.

I am Jesus the *Only Wise God* who knows everything that's ever happened. I know things that haven't yet happened and "calleth those things which are not as though they were" (Romans 4:17, *KJV*). I know what will happen to you before it happens, and I know the things that could have happened to you but didn't. Trust Me to guide you and protect you. Let Me help you make good decisions and keep you from physical harm and spiritual danger.

> *Lord Jesus, You know the future, and I don't know what will happen to me. So, guide me this day. You have kept me from making mistakes in the past, and You've protected me from evil. You are the Only Wise God. I need Your wise guidance to keep me from making mistakes. I will depend upon Your guidance this day. Amen.*

Reading: Psalm 39

Key Thought: My wisdom can help you make good decisions.

77
I Am Jesus the Prince of the Kings of the Earth

And from Jesus Christ...the prince of the kings of the earth.
—Revelation 1:5, KJV

I am Jesus *The Prince of the Kings of the Earth*. A prince is one who is waiting for the throne that he will formally assume in the future. I am Jesus the *Prince* who will assume My throne at My second return. Then I will be "King of Kings, and Lord of Lords" (Revelation 19:16). However, My future reign doesn't deny My present rulership in the hearts of My followers, or My sovereignty in Heaven. I want to sit on the throne of your heart.

Jesus, I pray, "Your kingdom come" (Matthew 6:10), for the future millennium. But for today, I want You to rule my heart.

I am Jesus the *Prince of the Kings of the Earth*. But now, in My sovereign plan, I allow each earthly ruler to rule. Whereas many earthly leaders ignore Me and violate My laws, still "the powers [rulers] that be are ordained of the Father" (Romans 13:1, *KJV*). Those who rebel at My authority will be punished when they stand before the judgment throne. Even when rulers rebel against the Father, He works His plans through them. Many rulers think they are doing whatever they want, but the Bible teaches, "The king's heart is in My hands…I turn it wherever I wish" (Proverbs 21:1).

Jesus, You have all power in Heaven and Earth. I marvel at Your patience and I praise You for working all things together for good to us who love You (See Romans 8:28). Amen.

Reading: John 17:1-19

Key Thought: Let Me rule your heart today because one day I'll rule all things.

78
I Am Jesus the Righteous Judge

Finally, there is laid up for me the crown of righteousness, which the Lord, the righteous Judge, will give to me on that Day.
—2 Timothy 4:8

I am Jesus the *Righteous Judge*. When you come into future judgment, I will not punish you for your sins, because I died for your sins. Your sins were judged on the cross (John 12:31-32; 16:11), and all your iniquities were covered by My blood. When you appear before *The Righteous Judge*, I will reward you for your faithfulness and service. Every good thing you've ever done will be evaluated by Me (See 1 Corinthians 3:13, 2 Corinthians 5:10). Then I'll give you your rewards, also called crowns (See James 1:12).

Jesus, You are The Righteous Judge. Thank You for forgiveness of sins. Thank You for mercy and grace. I don't deserve it, but I accept it.

I the *Righteous Judge* will not make mistakes when I judge people at the end of this age. Because I am omnipotent, with all power, I can bring every person and all facts into My presence. Because I am omnipresent, and omniscient, I know all things; I understand everyone's actions and motivations. Because I am God, you can count on Me to be a *Righteous Judge*. Whereas some corrupt judges can be bribed on this earth, I will give the right judgment in the right way. I will look at all the merits of your case when you appear before Me. You will get the appropriate rewards from Me the *Righteous Judge*.

> *Jesus, I know You are righteous, so I rest securely in Your presence. I know You will judge me rightly. Amen.*

Reading: 2 Timothy 4:1-16

Key Thought: I will give the right judgment in the right way.

79
I Am Jesus the Only Begotten of the Father

And the Word became flesh and dwelt among us, and we beheld His glory, the glory as of the only begotten of the Father, full of grace and truth.

—John 1:14

I am Jesus the *Only Begotten of the Father*. This means I came from the Father and I am the unique personification of the Father. I being begotten of the Father means that I am the expression of the Father. John 1:14 emphasizes My characteristics of being "the Word," which means that the message and meaning of the Word reflects the Father. When the Father wants to make an utterance to the world, He does it through Me, the Word.

Lord Jesus, I come asking You to teach me what the Father in Heaven is like. I want to love the Father more than ever, but I must know Him better to love Him better.

I am Jesus the *Only Begotten of the Father*. I am just like the Father. If you want to see what the Father looks like, look at Me in the Scriptures. If you want to know how the Father relates to you, look at how I relate to people. If you want to approach the Father, go to Him through Me. To know the Father better, know Me.

Lord Jesus, I look to You to see the Father. I know the father is Loving, because I see how You loved people. I know the Father is Powerful, because I see Your awesome power in creating the universe and in transforming individuals. I know the Father is kind and gentle, because You are patient with me and forgiving toward me. Amen.

Reading: John 1:14-28

Key Thought: To better know the Father, learn about Me.

80
I Am Jesus the Light of the Glorious Gospel

The god of this world hath blinded the minds of them which believe Not [the unsaved], *lest the light of the glorious gospel of Christ, who is the image of God, should shine unto them.*
—2 Corinthians 4:4, KJV

I am Jesus the *Light of the Glorious Gospel*. Did you see those two words, "Light" and "Glorious"? I am both the Light of the gospel and the Glory of the gospel. In a world where people are blinded by sin and where people are lost in the blackness of eternal night, I am the Light of salvation; I am the Light of the Gospel.

Lord Jesus, when I saw the Light, I believed. When the Light appeared in my life, I followed it. Give me more illumination today as I continue to walk where You lead.

I am Jesus the *Glory of the Gospel*. When the Shekinah glory cloud rested on the Ark of the Covenant, the priest had to leave the holy of holies (See Exodus 40:35; 2 Chronicles 5:14). Humans couldn't remain in My presence, i.e., the glory of God. Just as I came to dwell among Israel as the glory cloud, now I come to live in your life. It is through you and other followers that I bring the light of the gospel to the world. It is not just light that the Father wants unsaved people to see. He wants to bring the light of My presence into the hearts of unsaved people, so they can believe the glorious gospel. Remember that I said, "I am the light of the world" (John 8:12).

Lord Jesus, thank You for living in my heart. Shine Your Light to the world through me. I want to shine for You, the Light of the Glorious Gospel, to all people. Amen.

Reading: 2 Corinthians 4:1-6

Key Thought: I am the *Light* that gets people saved.

81
I Am Jesus the Light of the Knowledge of the Glory of God

For it is God who commanded light to shine out of darkness, who has shone in your heart to give the light of the knowledge of the glory of God in the face of Jesus Christ.
—2 Corinthians 4:6

I am Jesus the *Light of the Knowledge of the Glory of God.* Just as the Father shined out of darkness to give the world physical light, so I will shine into your darkened hearts to give spiritual light concerning Myself and My kingdom. Those who are blinded by sin live in a darkened world. They can't find their way to Heaven; they live in a black, cold and threatening world. Blinded people are shut up to their own limited experience; they are lost and without hope. But I came to give them the light of salvation. "I am the true Light who gives light to every one coming into the world" (John 1:9).

Jesus, it feels good to live where there's spiritual light. I can see spiritual things because of You. You have shown me how to live and what will happen to me when I die. Your Light is warm and comfortable, and I am confident of the future.

I am Jesus the *Light of the Knowledge of the Glory of God.* I shine light on unredeemed cultures, which are lost in the darkness of self-worship and greed. I help spiritually blinded people see the plan of salvation. I shines light on the pathway to guide My followers. I put a fire in their souls to give them hope for eternity.

> *Jesus, I love to walk in Your Light, because I remember how awful I felt walking in darkness. I will walk in Your Light for the rest of my life. Amen.*

Reading: 2 Corinthians 4

Key Thought: I am the Light that shows people where to walk.

82
I Am Jesus the Lion of the Tribe of Judah

One of the elders said to me, "Do not weep. Behold, the Lion of the tribe of Judah, the Root of David, has prevailed to open the scroll and to loose its seven seals."

—Revelation 5:5

I am Jesus the *Lion of the Tribe of Judah.* I fulfilled the Old Testament prediction of the King-Messiah (See Genesis 49:8-9) who would come from the tribe of Judah. Just as the lion is called the ruler of the jungle, so the lion symbol is used to describe earthly rulers. I am pictured as a lion because I will rule all mankind. Let Me rule your heart and lead you to a better life.

Jesus, come rule my heart, because I cannot rule it. Sometimes I don't do the things I want to do, and sometimes I do the things I don't want to do (See Romans 7:15).

I am Jesus the *Lion of the Tribe of Judah* who will prevail in the future to open the book and loose the seals (See Revelation 5:5). So, I can prevail against your unruly heart. I can rule your life and help you control your desires. I can keep you from excesses and lawlessness. But you must yield to Me so that I can control your life. Just as John was counseled not to weep because he couldn't open the book, so you shouldn't despair because of your weaknesses. I am the *Lion of the Tribe of Judah*; I have strength to help control your life today.

> *Jesus, I surrender my rebellious spirit to You, but I also want You to give me the power to do the will of the Father. When I lack inner strength and fortitude, I look to Your strength. I yield to Your rule for this day. Amen.*

Reading: Revelation 5:1-5

Key Thought: I can give you strength to control your weaknesses.

83
I Am Jesus the Lord of Glory

None of the rulers of this age knew; for had they known, they would not have crucified the Lord of glory.

—1 Corinthians 2:8

I am Jesus the *Lord of Glory*. I left Heaven and its glories to be born as a babe in Bethlehem. Heaven was magnified by My presence, but I gave up its luster and glory to be born in a humble stable and to be part of a poor family. When I left the side of the Father to come to Earth, I was the Lord *from* Glory. I gave it all up because of My love for fallen humanity. I am the *Lord of Glory* who came to die for the world.

Jesus, thank You for giving up Your heavenly home to come to Earth for sinners like me. Thank You for giving up Your glory to suffer the agonies of Calvary for me.

I left the glories of Heaven, knowing I would return. The night before I died, I prayed, "Glorify thou me with thine own self with the glory which I had with thee before the world was" (John 17:5, *KJV*) I am the Lord *from* Glory, but when I returned to Heaven, I had more glory than when I left. I had added My glorious victory over sin, death and the Evil One. Now I am truly the *Lord of Glory*. I have more glory now than before I came to the world.

Jesus, I want my life to add even more glory to You, for all You've done for me. I can't fully understand Your love, but I accept it. I glorify You because You alone are worthy of glory. Amen.

Reading: Philippians 2:1-11

Key Thought: I receive additional glory for My accomplishments on Calvary.

84
I Am Jesus the Lord of Peace

Now may the Lord of peace himself give you peace always in every way.
—2 Thessalonians 3:16

I am Jesus the *Lord of Peace*. As Lord I am Master so I am the *Master of Peace. My* nature is peace, so when I awoke in a boat in the middle of a violent storm, I commanded the winds, "Peace be still" (Mark 4:39). When I died on the cross for your sins, I made peace between the Father and you. Now because I am the Lord of Peace you can have peace with My Father (Romans 5:1). Since you are a Christian, I can calm your fears and so the your anxieties. I can give you the "peace of God" (See Philippians 4:7). Do you need My peace in our heart today?

Jesus, I come to You. Thank You for saving me and giving me peace with the Father. Thank You for living in my heart to give me the peace of salvation. Come be the Master of my heart.

I am Jesus the *Lord of Peace*. No other religious leader can give peace as I give, because peace of heart doesn't come from humans; it comes from the Father. No activity can give heart peace, unless it has Me as its focus. Money, fame, or earthly power cannot give you peace in this life or the life to come. If you want contentment, satisfaction, and deep inner joy, come to Me. I am the *Lord of Peace.*

> *Lord Jesus, I need Your peace to settle my fears for this day. Take control of my thinking and settle my mind. Help me look at life through Your perspective. Amen.*

Reading: Ephesians 2:11-22

Key Thought: I can give you peace because I am the *Lord of Peace.*

85
I Am Jesus, the Man Christ Jesus

For there is one God and one Mediator between God and men, the Man Christ Jesus.
—1 Timothy 2:5

I was human because I was born of the Virgin Mary. I am the *Man Christ Jesus;* therefore I understand your desires and dreams, and I know the weaknesses of the human body. I know what it means to be tired; I suffered on Calvary until I lost consciousness. You do not have any natural human weakness that I don't understand. Therefore, I, the *Man Christ Jesus* can intercede to the Father for you. I can ask for help for your weaknesses. Because I am a man, I can be your Mediator.

Christ Jesus, I come to You as my Mediator. You know my weaknesses and You understand my failures; ask the Father to give me strength to stand against temptation. You understand my dreams and ambitions; help me reach my life goals.

I am the *Man Christ Jesus.* When the title "Christ" appears before My human name "Jesus," it emphasizes My work on the cross as your Redeemer. When My name "Jesus" appears first, it emphasizes my humanity who died on the cross. So in today's verse, the *Man Christ* I stand at the right hand of the Father as your Intercessor and Mediator (See Hebrews 7:24, 25). I am pleading with the Father to forgive your sins. Confess all your sins now and ask for forgiveness, because I the *Man Christ Jesus* am interceding to the Father for you.

Christ Jesus, I come asking for forgiveness of sins. Be my Mediator with the Father for me. Cleanse me and make me useable to serve You this day. Amen.

Reading: 1 Timothy 2:1-7

Key Thought: I am the man Christ Jesus who is your effective Mediator to the Father.

86
I Am Jesus the Judge of the Living and the Dead

And He commanded us to preach to the people, and to testify that it is He who was ordained by God to be Judge of the living and the dead.
—Acts 10:42

I am Jesus the *Judge of the Living and the Dead*. This means that I am the Judge of believers and non-believers, those who are living and those already dead. Those who believe in Me are saved (they have eternal life); and those who don't believe in Me are dead in trespasses and sins (See Ephesians 2:1 ff). I will judge believers to give them their rewards, and I will judge the unsaved to determine their punishment (See Revelation 20:11, 12). I am the Judge of all people; none can escape My scrutiny. Because you believe in Me, your sins have been forgiven. I will not punish you in judgment, but you will have to give an account of your faithfulness and works (See 1 Corinthians 3:12-17).

> *Lord, thank You for eternal life. Help me to serve You faithfully. I look forward to seeing You, not to receive Your anger, but to receive Your rewards.*

I am Jesus the *Judge of the Living and the Dead*; no one will escape My judgment throne. Some think that only those living when I return will be judged. No, I will raise all the dead to appear before Me with the living. I am the Judge of all souls in the universe; no one will be exempt. Plead My mercy today, so you won't meet My anger in the future.

> *Jesus, I know You have judged my sins on the cross; in appreciation I worship You. I know You will judge all unsaved people, so in gratitude I thank You for salvation. I know all people will appear before You; I am not perfect, so I will be judged. My only plea is Your righteousness. Amen.*

Reading: Acts 10:34-43

Key Thought: I will judge all people, both saved and unsaved.

87
I Am Jesus the King Eternal

Now to the King eternal, immortal, invisible, to God who alone is wise, be honor and glory forever and ever. Amen.
—1 Timothy 1:17

I am Jesus the *King Eternal*. Just as an earthly king rules his kingdom through his laws, so I rule the universe by My laws. I control the natural world through natural laws, and I allow earthly rulers to control the social and political life of people through their judicial laws. I recognize earthly judicial laws and call on all people to obey them (See Romans 13:1-7). I control the spiritual world through spiritual laws; it is through these laws that I want to direct your life.

Jesus, be my King; I want You to direct my life. Come sit upon the throne of my heart to rule it.

I am Jesus the *King Eternal*. I have always ruled the universe. Look at one of My natural laws, such as the law of gravity; break this law and you'll suffer the consequences. Because I allow the Evil One to act contrary to My spiritual laws does not mean I am not in control. I want all people to serve Me out of love, not coercion. Those who choose to follow Me will be rewarded. Those who reject My rule will be punished. Today, I am Lord of those who yield to Me; but in the future "every knee will bow…every tongue will confess that Jesus Christ is Lord" (Philippians 2:10, 11). Will you recognize Me today?

Lord Jesus, I bow to worship You as my King. I accept Your rule upon this earth and will serve You gladly. Amen.

Reading: Romans 13:1-7

Key Thought: I want to rule your life as your King.

88
I Am Jesus the Foundation Which Is Laid

For no other foundation can anyone lay than that which is laid, which is Jesus Christ.
—1 Corinthians 3:11

Some young people ask today, "WWJD?" (What Would Jesus Do?) There is no other foundation on which anyone can build a life than on My example. There is no other foundation for salvation than My death. Now I stand in Heaven at the right hand of the Father as your Intercessor. I plead forgiveness for your sins and ask for strength for you to resist temptations. I am the Foundation upon which you now relate to God the Father. Will you build your life upon Me?

Jesus, I build my life upon Your teaching, for no one else gives me truth. I stake my salvation upon Your death, for You are the only forgiveness of sin. I live my life in the power of Your indwelling, for You are my only protection against evil.

I am Jesus the *Foundation Which Is Laid*. I have done everything for you that needs to be done. When I cried, "It is finished," on the cross, I completed salvation for you and for all who call upon My name. Salvation has been completed, and the Foundation is now laid. Your responsibility is to build your Christian life on that solid

Foundation. You can trust Me, for the Foundation is trustworthy.

Jesus, I will look beyond my doubt and fears. I will stand securely upon the Foundation Which Is Laid; I rest securely in You. I will look to You as my example; I will live for You as my Lord. Amen.

Reading: 1 Corinthians 3

Key Thought: I am the Foundation for a successful life.

89
I Am Jesus, the Hope of Israel

Because for the hope of Israel I am bound with this chain.

—Acts 28:20

I am Jesus the *Hope of Israel*. My people—the Jewish people—have suffered throughout history. Because I have promised to bless Israel, the Evil One hates them, because he hates both the Father and Me. The Jews have been targeted for persecution by many human enemies: Nebuchadnezzar, Haman, Adolph Hitler, just to name a few. The Evil One has used human instruments against them, like King Herod, who tried to destroy Me as a baby. But in spite of everything, I am still the *Hope of Israel*. I died to forgive the sins of the world, including the sins of the Jews.

Lord Jesus, I marvel at the scope of history. You were born into this world to a Jewish virgin and grew up in a Jewish home and lived in the Jewish culture. In spite of all that Satan has done, You are still the Hope of Israel.

I will be the *Hope of Israel*. There is coming a future tribulation aimed at the people of Israel, but I will return to save them and all those who believe in Me. In that future day, I'll still be the *Hope of Israel*. Just as I am their Hope, I am also your Hope. Look to Me today.

Jesus, not only are You the Hope of Israel, You are my Hope. You have come to help me through many trials in the past. I trust You for continual deliverance in the future. Amen.

Reading: Genesis 12:1-3

Key Thought: I am both your Hope and the Hope of Israel.

90
I Am Jesus the Commander of the Hosts of the Lord

So He [Jesus] said, "No, but as Commander of the army of the Lord I have now come." And Joshua fell on his face to the earth and worshiped, and said to Him, "What does my Lord say to His servant?" Then the Commander of the Lord's army said to Joshua, "Take your sandal off your foot, for the place where you stand is holy." And Joshua did so.
—Joshua 5:14-15

I am Jesus the *Commander of the Hosts of the Lord*. When Joshua was surveying the apparently impregnable Jericho before attacking the city, I appeared to Joshua. Originally, Joshua thought I was a soldier, so he asked, "Are You for us or for our adversaries?" (Joshua 5:13). I was not on either side. I simply answered that I was *The Commander of the Hosts of the Lord*. Joshua fell on his face, calling Me, "my Lord" (v. 14). The answer to victory over Jericho was not getting Me on his side, but Joshua's getting on My side. When Joshua submitted to Me, he was given a divine strategy to win the battle (See 6:2-5).

Jesus, too often I beg You for help in my plans. Teach me to submit my plans to You. I want to be on Your side.

When I appeared to Joshua, it was a Christophany, an appearance of Me in the Old Testament. Because the Commander is Me, victory comes when you yield to My plans. Because I the Commander am over the angelic host, victory comes when you get heavenly power on your side. I the *Commander of the Hosts of the Lord* told Joshua to take off his shoes because he was on holy ground; likewise, you must worship to achieve victory.

> *Lord Jesus, I realize I'm in a spiritual battle. I want to join Your army; show me what to do. I want spiritual victory; send angelic hosts to help me. I want fellowship with You, so I worship You. Amen.*

Reading: Joshua 5:13-6:21

Key Thoughts: Since I am your Commander in battle, you must join My army.

91
I Am Jesus the Cloud

I don't want you to forget, dear brothers and sisters, what happened to our ancestors in the wilderness long ago. God guided all of them by sending a cloud that moved along ahead of them, and he brought them all safely through the waters of the sea on dry ground.
—1 Corinthians 10:1, NLT

I am a picture of the *Cloud* that led Israel through the wilderness (See Exodus 14:19). I knew what I was doing when Israel followed Me to a dead end at the Red Sea. There were mountains on both sides, and Pharaoh's army was chasing them from behind. There was no way across the sea. Why did I ever put them in such a dangerous position? So My people would look to Me. Have you ever been at a dead end? Perhaps I led you there to teach you the greatest lessons in life. You're never at a dead end by yourself. Don't fear, for I am behind you, keeping the enemy away. Don't panic, I have a solution; you can leave a dead end as a victor.

Jesus, too often I am problem-focused, not victory-focused. Teach me to look beyond my dead-end situations to see You at work in my life.

When you get to a dead end, do what Israel did. First, wait on Me. Perhaps I've stopped your progress so you can learn about your finiteness and My almighty power. Just as Israel didn't expect Me to roll back the sea, maybe you don't know yet how I'll solve your problems. Second, just as Moses lifted his rod for Israel to go forward, so I want you to walk forward through your obstacles. If I don't test your faith, you'll not trust My guidance.

> *Lord Jesus, thank You for the dead ends of my life that make me look to You. Today, I look to You and call on Your power to see me through my obstacles. It's good to get going again. Amen.*

Reading: Exodus 14:18-22

Key Thought: Look for My purpose when you come to a dead end.

92
I Am Jesus the Consolation of Israel

And behold, there was a man in Jerusalem whose name was Simeon, and this man was just and devout, waiting for the Consolation of Israel.
—Luke 2:25

I am the *Consolation of Israel*. The word "consolation" means comfort, Israel was waiting for the Father to send Me, the Messiah, to deliver them from oppression and suffering. They wanted Me to give them comfort. Many Jews in that day were looking for political deliverance from Rome. They were oppressed financially, socially and, to some degree, spiritually. They expected Me to free them from military bondage; then they would be comforted. Much of life is expectation and perception." Because the Jews expected the wrong kind of deliverance, they wrongly perceived who I was and what I came to do.

Lord Jesus, give me eyes to see You clearly, a clear mind to understand You properly and a willing heart to follow You gladly.

I did not come the first time to sit on a military throne in Jerusalem. I came to sit on the throne of the your heart and the heart of all My followers. My consolation is not outward, but inward. I came to rule people's thoughts and dreams, and give them courage. When I rule people's hearts, I control from within. I am the inner *Consolation of Is*rael, or the comforter of hearts. When I come a second time, I will conquer outwardly and rule from Jerusalem.

Lord Jesus, come rule my heart. You are the fulfillment of my dreams; You are my comfort from oppression and suffering. Amen.

Reading: Isaiah 40

Key Thought: I offer inner comfort to you.

93

I Am Jesus a Good Man

And there was much murmuring among the people concerning him: for some said, He is a good man: others said, Nay; but he deceiveth the people.

—John 7:12

As the Feast of Tabernacles approached, I was the main topic of discussion. The people wondered whether I would come to the feast because there were rumors that the Jewish leaders would arrest Me. I had broken their Sabbath laws, and I claimed to be God. Some said I was a *Good Man;* others didn't think so. Some said I was a prophet (See John 7:40); others knew I did miracles. Some thought I was in fact their Messiah (See v. 41). During My life, as in the world today, "there was a division among the people because of Him" (v. 43). Many theological liberals say that the Bible is not authoritative; if that were true, I would be only a mere man. Some historians say that I was only a good man; if that were true, they couldn't be saved by Me. The problem is that I am the Lord God who demands your loyalty and total love.

Lord Jesus, I recognize that You are the Son of God, the second Person of the Trinity. I bow to worship You as my Savior.

To say that I am a *Good Man* is a first step, but it's not enough to save you. It doesn't take much to acknowledge that I am good. It demands your total response to acknowledge that I am Lord. What must you do? "For if you confess with your mouth that I am Lord and believe in your heart that the Father raised Me from the dead, you will be saved" (Romans 10:9, NLT).

Jesus, I confess that You are much more than a Good Man; You are the Lord of the universe; You are my Savior. Amen.

Reading: John 7:1-13

Key Thought: It's not enough to recognize Me as a *Good Man*; I must be your Lord.

94
I Am Jesus the Lawgiver

There is one Lawgiver, who is able to save and to destroy. Who are you to judge another?
—James 4:12

I am Jesus the *Lawgiver*. I run the world through natural laws such as the law of gravity. No one can break these laws without suffering consequences. I also run the spiritual world through moral laws. Because no one has perfectly kept all laws, no one can enter Heaven. I fulfilled the Law in My death; I nailed the law to My Cross. No longer will broken laws keep you from going to Heaven (Colossians 2:14, 15). Christianity is not about keeping rules or laws; it's about knowing Me. When you please Me, you satisfy all the laws, for I created the laws; I am the *Lawgiver*.

> *Lord Jesus, it's sometimes hard to keep the laws, because I have a rebellious streak in my heart. Help me submit to You. Help me live by Your principles.*

Don't be just a law-keeper; these people are called legalists. Look behind laws to see their purpose, because My laws were given to point you to Me. I said the greatest law of all is to love Me with all your heart, and the second is to love your neighbor as yourself (See Matthew 22:37-40). When you follow Me the

Lawgiver and live by the meaning of My laws, you will have a worthwhile life.

> *Lord Jesus, forgive me for just keeping laws for legalistic purposes. Show me Your purpose behind Your laws. I love You with all my heart, my soul, and my mind. Show me the real meaning behind Your laws, and give me the right attitude to live by them. Give me the power to keep them. Amen.*

Reading: Matthew 22:35-40

Key Thought: Focus on Me, not impersonal laws.

95
I Am Jesus the Life

Jesus said to him, "I am the way, the truth, and the life. No one comes to the Father except through Me."
—John 14:6

I am Jesus the *Life*; I am the source of life. I embedded the world with My life when I created it (See Colossians 1:16). The smallest building block of the universe is the cell, made up of protons, neutrons, and electrons, all held together by My enormous power who "holds all creation together" (v. 17, *NLT*). I am also the Source of human life. The first parents were made in My image when My life was breathed into Adam and he became "a living being" (Genesis 2:7).

Lord Jesus, I thank You for life in my physical body. I thank You for food to eat, water to drink, and air to breathe. I thank You for mental and spiritual life.

I am Jesus the source of spiritual life. I am Jesus the *life* of God who was put to death, but I arose on the third day. I am "the resurrection and the life" (John 11:25). The apostle John was referring to Me when he wrote, "The life was manifested, and we have seen, and bear witness, and declare you that eternal life which was with the Father and was manifested to us" (1 John 1:2). Have you seen and received Me? I am life.

Lord Jesus, I have received Your life—eternal life—when I was saved. I get enlightened from reading the Scriptures. I experience renewed life when I fellowship with You in prayer. I worship You for heavenly life. Amen.

Reading: John 3:22-36

Key Thought: You get My *Life* when you receive Me into your life.

96
I Am Jesus the Lamb Slain from the Foundation of the World

All who dwell on the earth will worship…the Lamb slain from the foundation of the world.
—Revelation 13:8

As Israel faced the first Passover, "Moses called all the elders of Israel and said to them, 'Pick out and take lambs for yourselves according to your families'" (Exodus 12:21). Each father placed his hands on the head of the lamb to confess the sins of each family member. Their sins were transferred to the lamb, and then the lamb was killed. The lamb died instead of the family. I am "the lamb of the Father who takes away the sin of the world" (John 1:29). Since I am called the Father's Lamb, this suggests that He sent Me—His Lamb to die for the sin of the world. I am the *Lamb Slain from the Foundation of the World*.

Lord Jesus, thank You for dying for the world, but thank You most of all for dying for me.

It was a historical event when I—God's Son—died on the cross. But the Father is not limited by a calendar to keep time as humans. The Father is eternal without time. He has always loved you and has always planned to give Me, His Son, to die for your sins. I am the *Lamb Slain from the Foundation of the World*. At another place, the Bible reminds you, "You were not redeemed with corruptible things, like silver or gold,…but with My precious blood as of a lamb…foreordained before the foundation of the world, but was manifest in these last times for you" (1 Peter 1:18-20).

Lord Jesus, thank You for planning my salvation from the foundation of the world. Thank You for coming to die on a cross for me. Amen.

Reading: Isaiah 53:1-7

Key Thought: My sacrifice for sins was planned in ages past, but was accomplished on the cross.

97
I Am Jesus the Head of All Principality and Power

And you are complete in Him, who is the head of all principality and power.
—Colossians 2:10

I am Jesus the *Head of All Principalities and Power*. This means laws and authority originally came from Me. Because I am righteous, I want you to live by My righteous principles. These are the principles by which I rule the world—principles (laws) of nature, the principles by which governments exist or the ethical principles that guide human conduct and human relationships. Also, the spiritual principles of peace and brotherly kindness come from Me. Commit yourself to learning all you can about the laws of this world (which come from Me) so that you can understand how I guide and control all things.

Lord Jesus, teach me to live by Your principles so that I can please You and be like You. But, I know my weaknesses; give me power to live by Your principles.

I am Jesus the *Head of All Principality and Power*. The energy of laws and principles flowed into the natural world when I created everything in the beginning. The principles by which people live flowed into humanity when I created people in My image. The principles by which I sovereignly guide all things come from My power, for I am the *Head of All Principalities and Power*.

Lord Jesus, I want to live by Your principles because I don't know all things, teach me Your laws. Because I am weak, I need Your strength. Because I am needy, I come to You for help. Amen.

Reading: Psalm 119:1-16

Key Thought: Know My principles because they are the secret to successful living.

98
I Am Jesus, the Rock

And I also say to you that you are Peter, and on this rock I will build My church, and the gates of Hades shall not prevail against it.
—Matthew 16:18

I am Jesus the *Rock* on which the Church is built. Some have mistakenly thought in Matthew 16:18 I was applying the word "rock" to Peter. The name "Peter" is *Petros*, a reference to a small stone, perhaps like a pebble. The word "rock" that refers to Me in this verse is *petra,* a large rock, actually like a rock ledge that sticks out of a mountain. The confusion has come because both words came from the same root. Actually, the Church is built on Peter's statement "You are the Christ, the Son of the living God" (v. 16). The Church is not a dead institution, though some churches are dead. The Church is alive because it's built on Me, the Son of the living God. The Church is alive because it's made up of individuals who believe that I am the Son of God and they have accepted Me into their hearts.

Lord Jesus, I know the Church is grounded on You; You are the Rock. I get stability from You.

When the Church is built on Me, it is as solid as a rock. I am the original church planter and church builder, for I said, "I will build My church." Also, the Church is continually being built, for in the statement, "I will build" contains a future tense verb that means "continually being built." I'll do it today. Finally, the Church belongs to Me; I call it "My church." When you're in Me, you're in the Church; and when you're in Me, you're on the *Rock*.

> *Jesus, I know the Church is growing because it is continually being built. I know I am secure in You because the gate of Hades can't prevail against Your work. Amen.*

Reading: Matthew 16:13-28

Key Thought: The Church is being built by Me.

99
I Am Jesus the Redeemer

For I know that my Redeemer lives, and He shall stand at last on the earth.
—Job 19:25

I am the *Redeemer*. Before you were saved, you were owned by sin and the Devil, but I bought you with a special redemptive price. "You were not redeemed with…silver and gold…but with My precious blood, as of a lamb" (1 Peter 1:18, 19). I am your *Redeemer*, and now you belong to Me.

Jesus, I sometimes forget what I was before You saved me. Never let me forget how You redeemed me. Thank You for releasing me from the prison house of sin. I am no longer a slave of the Devil. How can I serve You?

I am your *Redeemer* because I took your curse. "Christ has redeemed us from the curse of the law, having become a curse for us" (Galatians 3:13). I was punished for your sin; you are no longer in bondage to sin—you are free! But as your *Redeemer*, I did more than pay the price to release you from bondage; I adopted you as a son, "I redeemed those who were under the law, that you might receive the adoption as sons" (4:5). Now you're a part of the Father's family; now you have a privileged position in My family. I, your *Redeemer*, I have taken you from being a slave to sin and made you a part of the Father's family.

> *Thank You, Redeemer, for not leaving me stranded in sin. Thank You for bringing me into Your family and adopting me as Your child. "Redemption" is a wonderful word. I enjoy my new position in You. Amen.*

Reading: Galatians 4:1-7

Key Thought: I redeemed you and made you a member of My family.

100
I Am Jesus the Head of the Body

And He is the head of the body, the church, who is the beginning, the firstborn from the dead, that in all things He may have the preeminence.
—Colossians 1:18

I am Jesus the *Head of the Body*; the One who gives direction to the Church. Just as a head does the thinking for the human body, so I can do your thinking today. Just as the head makes choices, so I can guide your decision-making processes today. Just as the head sees the surrounding world and hears things and appreciates the aroma of good things, so I am your contact with the spiritual world. I know what has happened to you in the past, and I know what will happen in the future. Let Me—your Head—guide you today. I know all that good encounters and evil experiences are headed your way. Look to Me—your Head—for guidance this day.

Lord Jesus, I worship You for being the Head of the Body, the Head of the Church. But I want more than knowledge about You. Come be the Head of my life.

When the head is removed, the body dies; for the body can't work, play, serve, or worship without the head. You need Me for everything you do. You need Me more than once a week on Sundays and more than once a day for revitalization. You need Me every minute of every hour. I, the *Head of the Body* am the secret of living.

> *Lord Jesus, be my eyes so I can see spiritual things. Be my ears so I can hear the Father's voice; help me smell the sweet aroma of Your presence. I crown You as the Head of my life. Amen.*

Reading: Revelation 22:1-5

Key Thought: I must be the Head of your life.

Appendix 1
Jesus: Names, Titles, Metaphors, Figures of Speech and Pictures of Jesus[1]

A

The Advocate with the Father (1 John 2:1)

An Alien unto My Mother's Children (Psalm 69:8)

Alive for Evermore (Revelation 1:18)

The All and in All (Colossians 3:11)

The Almighty Which Is (Revelation 1:8)

The Alpha and Omega (Revelation 1:8)

An Altar (Hebrews 13:10)

The Altogether Lovely (Song of Solomon 5:16)

The Amen (Revelation 3:14)

The Angel of God (Genesis 21:17)

The Angel of His Presence (Isaiah 63:9)

The Angel of the Covenant (Malachi 3:1)

The Angel of the Lord (Genesis 16:7)

The Anointed of God (1 Samuel 2:35; Psalm 2:2)

Another King (Acts 17:7)

The Apostle of Our Profession (Hebrews 3:1)

The Ark of the Covenant (Joshua 3:3)

The Arm of the Lord (Isaiah 53:1)

The Author of Eternal Salvation (Hebrews 5:9)

The Author of Our Faith (Hebrews 12:2)

B

The Babe of Bethlehem (Luke 2:12,16)

The Balm in Gilead (Jeremiah 8:22)

A Banner to Them That Fear Thee (Psalm 60:4)

The Bearer of Glory (Zechariah 6:13)

The Bearer of Sin (Hebrews 9:28)

The Beauties of Holiness (Psalm 110:3)

Before All Things (Colossians 1:17)

The Beginning (Colossians 1:18)

The Beginning and the Ending (Revelation 1:8)

The Beginning of the Creation of God (Revelation 3:14)

The Beloved (Ephesians 1:6)

My Beloved Son (Matthew 3:17)

The Better (Hebrews 7:7)

The Bishop of Your Souls (1 Peter 2:25)

The Blessed and Only Potentate (1 Timothy 6:15)

The Blessed for Evermore (2 Corinthians 11:31)

The Blessed Hope (Titus 2:13)

The Branch (Zechariah 3:8; 6:12)

Appendix 1

The Branch of the Lord (Isaiah 4:2)

The Branch of Righteousness (Jeremiah 33:15)

The Branch Out of His Roots (Isaiah 11:1)

The Bread of God (John 6:33)

The Bread of Life (John 6:35)

The Breaker (Micah 2:13)

The Bridegroom of the Bride (John 3:29)

The Bright and Morning Star (Revelation 22:16)

The Brightness of His Glory (Hebrews 1:3)

The Brightness of Thy Rising (Isaiah 60:3)

Our Brother (Matthew 12:50)

A Buckler (Psalm 18:30)

The Builder of the Temple (Zechariah 6:12-13)

A Bundle of Myrrh (Song of Solomon 1:13)

C

The Captain of the Hosts of the Lord (Joshua 5:14-15)

The Captain of Their Salvation (Hebrews 2:10)

The Carpenter (Mark 6:3)

The Carpenter's Son (Matthew 13:55)

A Certain Nobleman (Luke 19:12)

A Certain Samaritan (Luke 10:33)

The Chief Cornerstone (Ephesians 2:20; 1 Peter 2:6)

The Chief Shepherd (1 Peter 5:4)

The Chiefest Among Ten Thousand (Song of Solomon 5:10)

A Child Born (Isaiah 9:6)

The Child Jesus (Luke 2:27,43)

Child of the Holy Ghost (Matthew 1:18)

The Chosen of God (Luke 23:35, 1 Peter 2:4)

Chosen Out of the People (Psalm 89:19)

Christ (Matthew 1:16)

The Christ (1 John 5:1)

Christ a King (Luke 23:2)

Christ Come in the Flesh (1 John 4:2)

Christ Crucified (1 Corinthians 1:23)

Christ Jesus (Acts 19:4)

Christ Jesus Our Lord (2 Corinthians 4:5)

The Christ of God (Luke 9:20)

Christ Our Passover (1 Corinthians 5:7)

Christ Risen from the Dead (1 Corinthians 15:20)

Christ the Lord (Luke 2:11)

A Cleft of the Rock (Exodus 33:22)

Cloud (1 Corinthians 10:1)

A Cluster of Camphire (Song of Solomon 1:14)

A Column of Smoke (see Exodus 13:21)

The Comforter (John 14:16-18)

Appendix 1

The Commander of the Hosts of the Lord (Joshua 5:14-15)

A Commander to the People (Isaiah 55:4)

Conceived of the Holy Spirit (Matthew 1:20)

The Consolation of Israel (Luke 2:25)

The Corn of Wheat (John 12:24)

Counselor (Isaiah 9:6)

The Covenant of the People (Isaiah 42:6; 49:8)

The Covert from the Tempest (Isaiah 32:2)

The Covert of Thy Wings (Psalm 61:4)

The Creator (Romans 1:25)

A Crown of Glory (Isaiah 28:5)

D

My Darling (Psalm 22:20)

David (Matthew 1:17)

The Day (2 Peter 1:19)

The Daysman Between Us (Job 9:33)

The Dayspring from on High (Luke 1:78)

Daystar (2 Peter 1:19)

His Dear Son (Colossians 1:13)

That Deceiver (Matthew 27:63)

My Defense (Psalm 94:22)

The Deliverance of Zion (Joel 2:32)

My Deliverer (Psalm 40:17)

The Desire of All Nations (Haggai 2:7)

Despised by the People (Psalm 22:6)

The Dew of Israel (Hosea 14:5)

A Diadem of Beauty (Isaiah 28:5)

The Door (John 10:9)

The Door of the Sheep (John 10:7)

Dwelling Place (Psalm 90:1)

E

Mine Elect (Isaiah 42:1)

Eliakim (Isaiah 22:20)

Elijah (Matthew 16:14)

Emmanuel (Matthew 1:23)

The End of the Law (Romans 10:4)

The Ensign of the People (Isaiah 11:10)

Equal with God (Philippians 2:6)

The Eternal God (Deuteronomy 33:27)

That Eternal Life (1 John 1:2)

The Everlasting Father (Isaiah 9:6)

An Everlasting Light (Isaiah 60:19-20)

An Everlasting Name (Isaiah 63:12)

His Excellency (Job 13:11)

The Excellency of Our God (Isaiah 35:2)

Excellent (Psalm 8:1,9)

The Express Image of His Person (Hebrews 1:3)

F

The Face of the Lord (Luke 1:76)

The Fairer than the Children of Men (Psalm 45:2)

Faithful (1 Thessalonians 5:24)

Faithful and True (Revelation 19:11)

The Faithful and True Witness (Revelation 3:14)

A Faithful Creator (1 Peter 4:19)

A Faithful High Priest (Hebrews 2:17)

A Faithful Priest (1 Samuel 2:35)

The Faithful Witness (Revelation 1:5)

A Faithful Witness Between Us (Jeremiah 42:5)

A Faithful Witness in Heaven (Psalm 89:37)

My Father (Psalm 89:26)

The Feast (1 Corinthians 5:8)

My Fellow (Zechariah 13:7)

The Finisher of the Faith (Hebrews 12:2)

The First and the Last (Revelation 1:8)

The First Begotten (Hebrews 1:6)

The First Begotten of the Dead (Revelation 1:5; "The Firstborn from the Dead," *NKJV*)

The Firstborn (Hebrews 12:23)

The Firstborn Among Many Brethren (Romans 8:29)

The Firstborn of Every Creature (Colossians 1:15)

Her Firstborn Son (Luke 2:7)

The Firstfruit (Romans 11:16)

The Firstfruits of Them That Sleep (1 Corinthians 15:20)

A Flag (see Isaiah 11:10)

Flesh (John 1:14)

The Foolishness of God (1 Corinthians 1:25)

Foreordained before the Foundation of the World (1 Peter 1:20)

The Forerunner (Hebrews 6:20)

Fortress (Psalm 18:2).

The Foundation Which Is Laid (1 Corinthians 3:11)

The Fountain of Life (Psalm 36:9)

The Fountain of Living Waters (Jeremiah 17:13)

The Free Gift (Romans 5:15)

The Friend of Publicans and Sinners (Matthew 11:9; Luke 7:34)

A Friend That Sticketh Closer than a Brother (Proverbs 18:24)

The Fruit of the Earth (Isaiah 4:2)

The Fruit of Thy Womb (Luke 1:42)

Fullers' Soap (Malachi 3:2)

Appendix 1

G

The Gift of God (John 4:10)

A Gin (Isaiah 8:14)

A Glorious High Throne from the Beginning (Jeremiah 17:12)

A Glorious Name (Isaiah 63:14)

Glory (Haggai 2:7)

My Glory (Psalm 3:3)

The Glory as of the Only Begotten of the Father (John 1:14)

The Glory of God (Romans 3:23)

The Glory of His Father (Matthew 16:27; Mark 8:38)

God (Revelation 21:7)

God Blessed Forever (Romans 9:5)

Our God Forever and Ever (Psalm 48:14)

God in the Midst of Her (Psalm 46:5)

God Manifest in the Flesh (1 Timothy 3:16)

The God of Glory (Psalm 29:3)

The God of Israel (Psalm 59:5)

The God of Jacob (Psalm 46:7)

The God of My Life (Psalm 42:8)

The God of My Mercy (Psalm 59:10)

God of My Righteousness (Psalm 4:1)

God of My Salvation (Psalm 18:46; 24:5)

God of My Strength (Psalm 43:2)

God Who Avengeth Me (Psalm 18:47)

God Who Forgavest Them (Psalm 99:8)

God with Us (Matthew 1:23)

A Good Man (John 7:12)

Good Master (Matthew 19:16)

The Good Shepherd (John 10:11)

The Goodman of the House (Matthew 20:11)

The Governor Among Nations (Psalm 22:28)

Great (Jeremiah 32:18)

The Great God (Titus 2:13)

A Great High Priest (Hebrews 4:14)

A Great Light (Isaiah 9:2)

A Great Prophet (Luke 7:16)

The Great Shepherd of the Sheep (Hebrews 13:20)

Greater (1 John 4:4)

A Greater and More Perfect Tabernacle (Hebrews 9:11)

Greater than Jonah (Matthew 12:41)

Greater than Our Father Abraham (John 8:53,57-58

Greater than Our Father Jacob (John 4:12)

Greater than Solomon (Matthew 12:42)

Greater than the Temple (Matthew 12:6)

Guest (Luke 19:7)

Our Guide Even unto Death (Psalm 48:14)

The Guide of My Youth (Jeremiah 3:4)

The Guiltless (Matthew 12:7)

H

The Habitation of Justice (Jeremiah 50:7)

Harmless (Hebrews 7:26; "Blameless," NLT)

An He Goat (Proverbs 30:31)

The Head of All Principality and Power (Colossians 2:10)

The Head of Every Man (1 Corinthians 11:3)

The Health of My Countenance (Psalm 42:11)

The Head of the Body (Colossians 1:18)

The Head of the Corner (1 Peter 2:7)

The Heir (Mark 12:7)

Heir of All Things (Hebrews 1:2)

The Helper of the Fatherless (Psalm 10:14)

A Hen (Matthew 23:37)

The Hidden Manna (Revelation 2:17)

My Hiding Place (Psalm 32:7)

A Hiding Place from the Wind (Isaiah 32:2)

The High and Lofty One Who Inhabiteth Eternity (Isaiah 57:15)

An High Priest (Hebrews 5:5)

An High Priest After the Order of Melchizedek (Hebrews 5:10)

An High Priest Forever (Hebrews 6:20)

My High Tower (Psalm 18:2)

The Highest Himself (Psalm 87:5)

An Highway (Isaiah 35:8)

Holy (Isaiah 57:15)

Thy Holy Child Jesus (Acts 4:27; "Your Holy Servant," NKJV)

The Holy One (Acts 2:27)

The Holy One and Just (Acts 3:14)

The Holy One of Israel (Psalm 89:18)

That Holy Thing Which Shall Be Born of Thee (Luke 1:35)

Holy to the Lord (Luke 2:23)

Our Hope (1 Timothy 1:1)

The Hope of Glory (Colossians 1:27)

The Hope of His People (Joel 3:16)

The Hope of Israel (Acts 28:20)

The Hope of Their Fathers (Jeremiah 50:7)

The Horn of David (Psalm 132:17)

A Horn of Salvation (Luke 1:69)

The Horn of the House of Israel (Ezekiel 29:21)

A House of Defense (Psalm 31:2)

A Householder (Matthew 20:1)

Her Husband (Revelation 21:2)

I

I AM (John 18:6)

The Image of the Invisible God (Colossians 1:15)

Immanuel (Isaiah 7:14)

Innocent Blood (Matthew 27:4)

Intercessor (Hebrews 7:24-25)

Isaac (Hebrews 11:17-18)

J

The Jasper Stone (Revelation 4:3)

Jeremiah (Matthew 16:14)

Jesus (Matthew 1:21)

Jesus Christ (Hebrews 13:8)

Jesus Christ the Lord (Romans 7:25)

Jesus Christ, the Son of God (John 20:31)

Jesus of Galilee (Matthew 26:69)

Jesus of Nazareth (John 1:45)

Jesus of Nazareth, the King of the Jews (John 19:19)

A Jew (John 4:9)

John the Baptist (Matthew 16:14)

Joseph's Son (Luke 4:22)

The Judge of the Quick and the Dead (Acts 10:42; "The Judge of the Living and the Dead," NKJV)

A Judge of the Widows (Psalm 68:5)

The Just One (Acts 7:52)

This Just Person (Matthew 27:24)

K

Thy Keeper (Psalm 12:15)

The Kindness and Love of God (Titus 3:4)

The King Eternal (1 Timothy 1:17)

The King Forever and Ever (Psalm 10:16)

The King Immortal (1 Timothy 1:17)

The King in His Beauty (Isaiah 33:17)

The King Invisible (1 Timothy 1:17)

The King of All the Earth (Psalm 47:7)

The King of Glory (Psalm 24:7-8)

The King of Heaven (Daniel 4:37)

The King of Israel (John 1:49)

King of Kings and Lord of Lords (Revelation 19:16)

The King of Peace (Hebrews 7:2)

The King of Righteousness (Hebrews 7:2)

King of Saints (Revelation 15:3)

Appendix 1

The King of Salem (Hebrews 7:2)

The King of Terrors (Job 18:14)

King of the Jews (Matthew 2:2)

The King Who Cometh in the Name of the Lord (Luke 19:38)

The King's Son (Psalm 72:1)

The Kinsman (Ruth 4:14)

L

A Ladder (Genesis 28:12)

The Lamb (Revelation 17:14)

The Lamb of God (John 1:29)

The Lamb Slain from the Foundation of the World (Revelation 13:8)

The Lamb That Was Slain (Revelation 5:12)

The Lamb Who Is in the Midst of the Throne (Revelation 7:17)

The Last (Isaiah 44:6)

The Last Adam (1 Corinthians 15:45)

The Lawgiver (James 4:12)

A Leader (Isaiah 55:4)

The Life (John 14:6)

A Life-Giving Spirit (1 Corinthians 15:45)

The Lifter Up of Mine Head (Psalm 3:3)

The Light (John 1:7)

The Light of the City (Revelation 21:23)

The Light of the Glorious Gospel of Christ (2 Corinthians 4:4)

The Light of the Knowledge of the Glory of God (2 Corinthians 4:6)

The Light of Men (John 1:4)

The Light of the Morning (2 Samuel 23:4)

The Light of the World (John 8:12)

The Light of Truth (Psalm 43:3)

A Light to Lighten Gentiles (Luke 2:32)

A Light to the Gentiles (Isaiah 49:6)

The Lily Among Thorns (Song of Solomon 2:2)

The Lily of the Valleys (Song of Solomon 2:1)

The Lion of the Tribe of Judah (Revelation 5:5)

The Living Bread (John 6:51)

The Living God (Psalm 42:2)

Lord (*despotes*; 2 Peter 2:1)

Lord (*kurios*; John 13:13)

Lord (*rabboni*; Mark 10:51)

Lord Also of the Sabbath (Mark 2:28)

My Lord and My God (John 20:28)

The Lord and Savior (2 Peter 1:11)

Lord Both of the Dead and Living (Romans 14:9)

The Lord from Heaven (1 Corinthians 15:47)

Appendix 1

Lord God Almighty (Revelation 16:7)

Lord God of Israel (Psalm 41:13)

The Lord God of the Holy Prophets (Revelation 22:6)

Lord God of Truth (Psalm 31:5)

Lord God Omnipotent (Revelation 19:6)

The Lord God Who Judgeth Her (Revelation 18:8)

The Lord Holy and True (Revelation 6:10)

Lord Jesus (Romans 10:9)

Lord Jesus Christ (James 2:1)

The Lord of All the Earth (Joshua 3:11)

The Lord of Glory (1 Corinthians 2:8)

The Lord of Hosts (Psalm 24:10)

Lord of Lords (1 Timothy 6:15)

Lord of Peace (2 Thessalonians 3:16)

The Lord of the Vineyard (Matthew 20:8)

The Lord of the Whole Earth (Psalm 97:5)

O Lord Our God (Psalm 8:1,9)

The Lord Strong and Mighty (Psalm 24:8)

The Lord Who Is and Who Was and Who Is to Come (Revelation 1:8, *NKJV*)

The Lord's Christ (Revelation 11:15)

The Lord's Doing (Matthew 21:42)

Lowly in Heart (Matthew 11:29)

M

Magnified (Psalm 40:16)

Our Maker (Psalm 95:6)

A Malefactor (John 18:30)

The Man (John 19:5)

A Man Approved of God (Acts 2:22)

A Man Child (Revelation 12:5)

The Man Christ Jesus (1 Timothy 2:5)

A Man Gluttonous (Matthew 11:19)

The Man of Sorrows (Isaiah 53:3)

The Man Whom He Hath Ordained (Acts 17:31)

The Man Whose Name Is the Branch (Zechariah 6:12)

Manna (Exodus 16:15)

Marvelous in Our Eyes (Matthew 21:42)

The Master *(didaskalos;* John 11:28)

Master *(epistates;* Luke 5:5)

Your Master *(kathegetes;* Matthew 23:10)

Master *(rabbi;* John 4:31)

The Master of the House *(oikodespotes;* Luke 13:25)

The Meat Offering (Leviticus 2:1)

The Mediator (1 Timothy 2:5)

The Mediator of a Better Covenant (Hebrews 8:6)

Appendix 1

The Mediator of the New Covenant
(Hebrews 12:24)

The Mediator of the New Testament
(Hebrews 9:15)

Meek (Matthew 11:29)

Melchizedek (Genesis 14:18)

A Merciful and Faithful High Priest (Hebrews 2:17)

His Mercy and His Truth (Psalm 57:3)

Mercy Seat (Hebrews 9:5; 1 John 2:2)

Messenger of the Covenant (Malachi 3:1)

Messiah (Daniel 9:26)

Messiah the Prince (Daniel 9:25)

Mighty (Psalm 89:19)

The Mighty God (Isaiah 9:6)

The Mighty One of Jacob (Isaiah 49:26; 60:16)

The Minister of Sin (Galatians 2:17)

A Minister of the Circumcision (Romans 15:8)

The Minister of the Heavenly Sanctuary
(Hebrews 8:1-3)

A More Excellent Name (Hebrews 1:4)

The Morning Star (Revelation 2:28)

The Most High (Psalm 9:2; 21:7)

The Mouth of God (Matthew 4:4)

The Mystery of God (Colossians 2:2)

N

A Nail Fastened in a Sure Place (Isaiah 22:23)

A Name Above Every Name (Philippians 2:9)

A Name for Salvation (John 20:31)

A Name No Man Knew (Revelation 19:12)

Name of Jesus (Colossians 3:17)

A Nazarene (Matthew 2:23)

Thy New Name (Revelation 3:12)

A Nourisher of Thine Old Age (Ruth 4:15)

O

An Offering and a Sacrifice to God (Ephesians 5:2)

The Offspring of David (Revelation 22:16)

Ointment Poured Forth (Song of Solomon 1:3)

The Omega (Revelation 22:13)

One of the Prophets (Matthew 16:14)

The Only Begotten of the Father (John 1:14)

His Only Begotten Son (John 3:16)

Only Potentate (1 Timothy 6:15)

The Only Wise God (1 Timothy 1:17)

An Owl of the Desert (Psalm 102:6)

P

Our Passover (1 Corinthians 5:7)

Appendix 1

The Path of Life (Psalm 16:11)

A Pavilion (Psalm 31:20)

Our Peace (Ephesians 2:14)

The Peace Offering (Leviticus 3:1)

A Pelican of the Wilderness (Psalm 102:6)

A Perfect Man (James 3:2)

The Person of Christ (2 Corinthians 2:10)

Physician (Luke 4:23)

The Place of Our Sanctuary (Jeremiah 17:12)

A Place of Refuge (Isaiah 4:6)

A Plant of Renown (Ezekiel 34:29)

A Polished Staff (Isaiah 49:2)

Poor (2 Corinthians 8:9)

My Portion (Psalm 119:57)

The Portion of Jacob (Jeremiah 51:19)

The Portion of Mine Inheritance (Psalm 16:5)

The Potter (Jeremiah 18:6)

The Power of God (1 Corinthians 1:24)

Praying in My Name (John 14:14)

Precious (1 Peter 2:7)

A Precious Cornerstone (Isaiah 28:16)

The Preeminence (Colossians 1:18)

A Price (1 Corinthians 6:20)

The Price of His Redemption (Leviticus 25:52)

A Priest Forever (Psalm 110:4)

The Priest of the Most High God (Hebrews 7:1)

A Prince and Savior (Acts 5:31)

The Prince of Life (Acts 3:15)

Prince of Peace (Isaiah 9:6)

Prince of Princes (Daniel 8:25)

The Prince of the Kings of the Earth (Revelation 1:5)

The Prophet (John 7:40)

A Prophet Mighty in Deed and Word (Luke 24:19)

The Prophet of Nazareth (Matthew 21:11)

A Prophet Without Honor (Matthew 13:57)

Propitiation (1 John 2:1-2)

Pure (1 John 3:3)

A Purifier of Silver (Malachi 3:3)

Q

Of Quick Understanding (Isaiah 11:3)

A Quickening Spirit (1 Corinthians 15:45)

R

Rabbi (John 3:2)

Rabboni (John 20:16)

Rain upon the Mown Grass (Psalm 72:6)

A Ransom for All (1 Timothy 2:6)

Appendix 1

A Ransom for Many (Matthew 20:28)

The Red Heifer Without Spot (Numbers 19:2)

My Redeemer (Job 19:25)

Redemption (1 Corinthians 1:30; Luke 21:28)

The Redemption of Their Souls (Psalm 49:8)

A Refiner's Fire (Malachi 3:2)

Our Refuge (Psalm 46:1)

A Refuge for the Oppressed (Psalm 9:9)

A Refuge from the Storm (Isaiah 25:4)

A Refuge in Times of Trouble (Psalm 9:9)

Our Report (Isaiah 53:1)

A Reproach of Men (Psalm 22:6)

Their Resting Place (Jeremiah 50:6)

A Restorer of Thy Life (Ruth 4:15)

Resurrection (John 11:25)

The Revelation of Jesus Christ (Revelation 1:1)

Reverend (Psalm 111:9)

A Reward for the Righteous (Psalm 58:11)

Rich (Romans 10:12)

The Riches of His Glory (Romans 9:23)

The Riddle (Judges 14:14)

Right (Deuteronomy 32:4)

The Righteous (1 John 2:1)

A Righteous Branch (Jeremiah 23:5)

The Righteous God (Psalm 7:9)

The Righteous Judge (2 Timothy 4:8)

The Righteous Lord (Psalm 11:7)

A Righteous Man (Luke 23:47)

My Righteous Servant (Isaiah 53:11)

Righteousness (1 Corinthians 1:30)

The Righteousness of God (Romans 10:3)

A River of Water in a Dry Place (Isaiah 32:2)

The Rock (Matthew 16:18)

The Rock of His Salvation (Deuteronomy 32:15)

The Rock of Israel (2 Samuel 23:3)

The Rock of My Refuge (Psalm 94:22)

A Rock of Offense (Romans 9:33)

The Rock of Our Salvation (Psalm 95:1)

Rock of Spiritual Refreshment (1 Corinthians 10:4, TLB)

The Rock of Thy Strength (Isaiah 17:10)

The Rock That Is Higher than I (Psalm 61:2)

The Rod (Micah 6:9)

A Rod Out of the Stem of Jesse (Isaiah 11:1)

The Root and Offspring of David (Revelation 22:16)

The Root of David (Revelation 5:5)

Appendix 1

A Root of Jesse (Isaiah 11:10; Romans 15:12)

A Root Out of Dry Ground (Isaiah 53:2)

The Rose of Sharon (Song of Solomon 2:1)

A Ruler (Micah 5:2)

S

The Sacrifice for Sins (Hebrews 10:12)

A Sacrifice to God (Ephesians 5:2)

My Salvation (Psalm 27:1)

The Salvation of God (Luke 2:30; 3:6)

The Salvation of Israel (Jeremiah 3:23)

A Samaritan (John 8:48)

The Same Yesterday, Today and Forever (Hebrews 13:8)

A Sanctuary (Isaiah 8:14)

A Sardius Stone (Revelation 4:3)

The Saving Strength of His Anointed (Psalm 28:8)

Saviour (Titus 2:13)

The Saviour of All Men (1 Timothy 4:10)

The Saviour of the Body (Ephesians 5:23)

The Saviour of the World (John 4:42; 1 John 4:14)

The Scapegoat (Leviticus 16:8; John 11:49-52)

The Sceptre of Israel (Numbers 24:17)

The Sceptre of Thy Kingdom (Psalm 45:6)

The Second Man (1 Corinthians 15:47)
Secret (Judges 13:18)
The Secret of Thy Presence (Psalm 31:20)
The Seed of Abraham (Galatians 3:16)
The Seed of David (Romans 1:3; 2 Timothy 2:8)
The Seed of the Woman (Genesis 3:15)
The Sent One (John 9:4)
Separate from His Brethren (Genesis 49:26)
Separate from Sinners (Hebrews 7:26)
The Serpent in the Wilderness (John 3:14)
My Servant (Isaiah 42:1)
A Servant of Rulers (Isaiah 49:7)
My Servant the Branch (Zechariah 3:8)
A Shadow from the Heat (Isaiah 25:4)
The Shadow of a Great Rock (Isaiah 32:2)
The Shadow of the Almighty (Psalm 91:1)
A Shelter (Psalm 61:3)
My Shepherd (Psalm 23:1; Isaiah 40:11)
Shepherd of Israel (Psalm 80:1)
Our Shield (Psalm 84:9)
Shiloh (Genesis 49:10)
Shoshannim (titles of Psalm 45; 69)
A Sign of the Lord (Isaiah 7:11)

Appendix 1

Siloam (John 9:7)

Sin (2 Corinthians 5:21)

A Snare to the Inhabitants of Jerusalem (Isaiah 8:14)

The Son (Matthew 11:27)

God's Son from Heaven (1 Thessalonians 1:10)

A Son Given (Isaiah 9:6)

The Son of Abraham (Matthew 1:1)

The Son of David (Mark 10:47)

The Son of God (John 1:49)

The Son of Joseph (John 1:45)

The Son of Man (John 1:51)

The Son of Mary (Mark 6:3)

The Son of the Blessed (Mark 14:61)

The Son of the Father (2 John 3)

The Son of the Freewoman (Galatians 4:30)

The Son of the Highest (Luke 1:32)

The Son of the Living God (Matthew 16:16)

The Son of the Most High (Mark 5:7)

A Son over His Own House (Hebrews 3:6)

The Son Who Is Consecrated for Evermore (Hebrews 7:28)

My Song (Isaiah 12:2)

The Sower (Matthew 13:4,37)

A Sparrow Alone upon the House Top (Psalm 102:7)

That Spiritual Rock (1 Corinthians 10:4)

A Star Out of Jacob (Numbers 24:17)

My Stay (Psalm 18:18)

A Stone Cut Out of the Mountain (Daniel 2:45)

A Stone Cut Without Hands (Daniel 2:34)

The Stone of Israel (Genesis 49:24)

A Stone of Stumbling (1 Peter 2:8)

The Stone Which the Builders Refused (Psalm 118:22)

The Stone Which the Builders Rejected (Matthew 21:42)

The Stone Which Was Set at Nought (Acts 4:11)

A Stranger (Matthew 25:35)

My Strength (Isaiah 12:2)

The Strength of Israel (1 Samuel 15:29)

The Strength of My Life (Psalm 27:1)

A Strength to the Needy in Distress (Isaiah 25:4)

A Strength to the Poor (Isaiah 25:4)

Strong (Psalm 24:8)

A Strong Consolation (Hebrews 6:18)

A Strong Lord (Psalm 89:8)

My Strong Refuge (Psalm 71:7)

Appendix 1

My Strong Rock (Psalm 31:2)

A Strong Tower (Proverbs 18:10)

A Strong Tower from the Enemy (Psalm 61:3)

A Stronger than He (Luke 11:22)

A Stronghold in the Day of Trouble (Nahum 1:7)

A Stumbling Block (1 Corinthians 1:23)

The Sun of Righteousness (Malachi 4:2)

A Sure Foundation (Isaiah 28:16)

The Sure Mercies of David (Isaiah 55:3; Acts 13:34)

The Surety of a Better Testament (Hebrews 7:22; "The Surety of a Better Covenant," *NKJV*)

A Sweet-Smelling Savor (Ephesians 5:2; "A Sweet-Smelling Aroma," *NKJV*)

T

A Tabernacle for a Shadow (Isaiah 4:6)

The Tabernacle of God (Revelation 21:3)

Teacher (Matthew 10:25)

A Teacher Come from God (John 3:2)

The Temple (John 2:19)

The Tender Grass (2 Samuel 23:4)

The Tender Mercy of God (Luke 1:78)

A Tender Plant (Isaiah 53:2)

The Testator (Hebrews 9:16-17)

The Testimony of God (1 Corinthians 2:1)

This Treasure (2 Corinthians 4:7)

The Trespass Offering (Leviticus 5:6)

A Tried Stone (Isaiah 28:16)

The Triumphant Lamb (Revelation 5:6)

The Triumphant Son of Man (Revelation 1:12-13)

The True Bread from Heaven (John 6:32)

The True God (Jeremiah 10:10)

The True Light (John 1:9)

The True Vine (John 15:1)

The True Witness (Proverbs 14:25)

The Trustworthy Witness (Revelation 1:5, AMP)

The Truth (John 14:6)

U

Undefiled (Hebrews 7:26)

Understanding (Proverbs 3:19)

The Unspeakable Gift (2 Corinthians 9:15)

The Upholder of All Things (Hebrews 1:3)

Upright (Psalm 92:15)

The Urim and Thummin (Exodus 28:30)

V

The Veil (Hebrews 10:20)

Very Great (Psalm 104:1)

Appendix 1

A Very Present Help in Trouble (Psalm 46:1)

The Victory (1 Corinthians 15:54)

The Vine (John 15:5)

The Voice (Revelation 1:12)

W

A Wall of Fire (Zechariah 2:5)

The Wave Offering (Leviticus 7:30)

The Way (John 14:6)

The Way of Holiness (Isaiah 35:8)

The Weakness of God (1 Corinthians 1:25)

A Wedding Garment (Matthew 22:12)

The Well of Salvation (Isaiah 12:3)

Wisdom (1 Corinthians 1:25)

The Wisdom of God (1 Corinthians 1:24)

A Wise Master Builder (1 Corinthians 3:10)

Witness (Judges 11:10)

My Witness (Job 16:19)

A Witness to the People (Isaiah 55:4)

Wonderful (Isaiah 9:6)

Wonderful Counselor (Isaiah 9:6)

The Word (John 1:1)

The Word of God (Revelation 19:13)

The Word of Life (1 John 1:1)

A Worm and No Man (Psalm 22:6)

Worthy (Revelation 4:11; 5:12)

That Worthy Name (James 2:7)

Worthy to Be Praised (Psalm 18:3)

X

X (an unknown quantity; see Revelation 19:12)

Y

The Yokefellow (Matthew 11:29-30)

The Young Child (Matthew 2:11)

Z

Zaphnath-Paaneah (Genesis 41:45)

The Zeal of the Lord of Hosts (Isaiah 37:32)

The Zeal of Thine House (Psalm 69:9; John 2:17)

Zerubbabel (Zechariah 4:7,9)

Note

1. Adapted from Elmer L. Towns, *The Names of Jesus* (Denver, CO: Accent Publications, 1987).

Appendix 2
Jesus: Preeminent Pronouns of Jesus in Scripture[1]

He That Cometh (Matthew 11:14; Luke 7:19)

He That Cometh After Me (John 1:15,27)

He That Cometh in the Name of the Lord (Matthew 21:9)

He That Cometh into the World (John 11:27)

He That Filleth All in All (Ephesians 1:23)

He That Hath the Bride (John 3:29)

He That Holdeth the Seven Stars (Revelation 2:1)

He That Is Higher than the Highest (Ecclesiastes 5:8)

He That Is Holy (Revelation 3:7)

He That Is True (Revelation 3:7)

He That Keepeth Israel (Psalm 121:4)

He That Liveth (Revelation 1:18)

He That Openeth (Revelation 3:7)

He That Sanctifieth (Hebrews 2:11)

He That Shutteth (Revelation 3:7)

He That Was Dead and Is Alive (Revelation 2:8)

He Who Brought Us Up (Joshua 24:17)

He Who Cometh Down from Heaven (John 6:33)

He Who Created (Revelation 10:6)

He Who Fighteth for You (Joshua 23:10)

He Who Hath His Eyes Like a Flame of Fire (Revelation 2:18)

He Who Hath His Feet Like Fine Brass (Revelation 2:18)

He Who Hath the Seven Spirits of God (Revelation 3:1)

He Who Hath the Sharp Sword with Two Edges (Revelation 2:12)

He Who Searcheth (Revelation 2:23)

He Who Sitteth in the Heavens (Psalm 2:4)

He Who Testifieth (Revelation 22:20)

He Who Walketh in the Midst of the Seven Candlesticks (Revelation 2:1)

Him That Bringeth Good Tidings (Nahum 1:15)

Him That Liveth Forever and Ever (Revelation 10:6)

Him That Loveth Us (Revelation 1:5)

Him That Sitteth on the Throne (Revelation 6:16)

Him That Was Valued (Matthew 27:9)

Him Who Is and Who Was and Who Is to Come (Revelation 1:4)

The One That Has the Key of David (Revelation 3:7)

This That Forgiveth Sins (Luke 7:49)

Thou Rulest the Raging of the Sea (Psalm 89:9)

Appendix 2

Thou Who Hearest Prayer (Psalm 65:2)

Thou Who Liftest Me Up from the Gates of Death (Psalm 9:13)

Thou Who Saveth by Thy Right Hand (Psalm 17:7)

Who Art, and Wast and Shalt Be (Revelation 16:5)

Who Coverest Thyself with Light (Psalm 104:2)

Who Crowneth Thee with Lovingkindness (Psalm 103:4)

Who Dwelleth in Zion (Psalm 9:11)

Who Forgiveth All Thine Iniquities (Psalm 103:3)

Who Girdeth Me with Strength (Psalm 18:32)

Who Giveth Me Counsel (Psalm 16:7)

Who Hast Power over These Plagues (Revelation 16:9)

Who Healeth All Thy Diseases (Psalm 103:3)

Who Laid the Foundations of the Earth (Psalm 104:5)

Who Layeth the Beams of His Chambers in the Waters (Psalm 104:3)

Who Maketh His Angels Spirits (Psalm 104:4; Hebrews 1:7)

Who Maketh the Clouds His Chariot (Psalm 104:3)

Who Redeemeth Thy Life from Destruction (Psalm 103:4)

Who Satisfieth Thy Mouth with Good Things (Psalm 103:5)

Who Saveth the Upright in Heart (Psalm 7:10)

Who Stretchest Out the Heavens Like a Curtain (Psalm 104:2)

Who Walketh upon the Wings of the Wind (Psalm 104:3)

Whom Thou Hast Sent (John 17:3)

Note

1. Taken from *365 Ways to Know God*, by Elmer Towns, Ventura, CA, Regal Books, Inc. 2004. Pages 393-394

Bio

Elmer L. Towns is Dean Emeritus of the School of Religion and Theological Seminary at Liberty University, which he cofounded in 1971 with Jerry Falwell. He continues to teach the Pastor's Bible Class at Thomas Road Baptist Church each Sunday, which is televised on a local network and Angel One.

Experience a personal revival!

Spirit-empowered content from today's top Christian authors delivered directly to your inbox.

Join today!
lovetoreadclub.com

Inspiring Articles
Powerful Video Teaching
Resources for Revival

Get all of this and so much more, e-mailed to you twice weekly!

LOVE TO READ CLUB
by **D** DESTINY IMAGE

www.ingramcontent.com/pod-product-compliance
Lightning Source LLC
Chambersburg PA
CBHW071404160426
42813CB00083B/444